The POWER Series
US NAVY
SEALS

Hans Halberstadt

Motorbooks International
Publishers & Wholesalers

For Miss Sarah Linda Horton,
a relative of mine with a fondness for
marine mammals.

First published in 1993 by Motorbooks
International Publishers & Wholesalers, PO Box 2,
729 Prospect Avenue, Osceola, WI 54020 USA

© Hans Halberstadt, 1993

Motorbooks International books are also available
at discounts in bulk quantity for industrial or sales-
promotional use. For details write to Special Sales
Manager at the Publisher's address

Library of Congress Cataloging-in-Publication Data

Halberstadt, Hans.
    US Navy SEALS / Hans Halberstadt.
       p.   cm. — (The Power series)
    Includes index.
    ISBN 0-87938-781-5
    1. United States. Navy. Sear, Air, Land
      Teams. 2. United States. Navy—
      Commando troops. I. Title. II. Series:
      Power series (Osceola, Wis.)
VG87.H35   1993
359.9—dc20   93-11367

On the front cover: A SEAL equipped with the
Draeger rebreathing system.

On the back cover: Top, SEALS come ashore from
their "rubber duck." Below, during BUD/S, the SEAL
trainees learn another use for the 250-pound
"rubber duck," holding it aloft for minutes at a time.

On the frontispiece page: Once ashore, the
SEALs operate like any other special operations
force.

On the title page: SEALs can spend a lot of time
lying in the surf, watching and waiting, during a
recon. This demonstration is done in daylight, but
real world ops are normally done at night.

Printed and bound in Hong Kong

Contents

Acknowledgments

Many thanks to the friendly folks at USSO-COM public affairs at MacDill Air Force Base, Florida, particularly Col. Jake Dye.

This book wouldn't have been attempted without the reassurance of RADM Brent Baker, now retired, former Navy Chief of Information, who responded very graciously to some criticism of mine with an invitation to try working with the Navy again. The result is this book. Sir, I salute you.

Another salute to LCDR John Brindley and JO1 Mike Hayden, as hard a pair of public affairs officers as you'll find anywhere, with one of the most difficult missions in the fleet—smack dab in the middle between the media maniacs and the Naval Special Warfare community (whose motto is *No pictures!!! No names!!! No kidding!!!*). To two fine people doing what is usually a thankless job, let me say: Thanks! Well done!

I'd like to personally thank the many folks at BUD/S and SEAL Teams Three and Five who helped so graciously, and against tradi-tion, with this project. I'd like to, but I can't. National Security and all that. But the Desert Patrol Vehicle guys out at Niland, California, and the squad from Team Five went way out of their way to accommodate a bunch of media weenies and executed their op with a perfect blend of cooperation and consideration.

I *can* thank RADM Ray Smith—what a guy! He's largely responsible for a new, more open attitude toward public affairs within the Naval Special Warfare community, and it's about time. A salute to you, sir, as well.

CAPT Bob Gormly, USN (Ret.), and CDR Gary Stubblefield, USN (Ret.), both filled in the gaps in my Naval Special Warfare education, shared some wonderful war stories and lots of insights based on long careers in Naval Special Warfare. These are, despite the reputation of the SEALs, gentlemen—the kind of quiet professionals you seldom hear about in this community. It's too bad that more Americans can't know about the things these people and their teams have done for us all.

Chapter 1

Let Slip the Frogs of War

In the dark, damp hours before midnight, 19 December 1989, a small group of United States Navy SEALs put the finishing touches on their face paint, checked their weapons and equipment for the thousandth time, watched the clock, chatted nervously, and waited. There were twenty-one of them, all told, assembled and identified as Task Unit Whiskey.

As the time trickled away all of them knew that very soon blood would begin to flow. Whose and how much remained to be seen. At 0045 hours, according to the current plan, combined United States forces would initiate Operation Just Cause—combat operations against the Republic of Panama with the objective of seizing that nation's leader, Gen. Manuel Noriega. Tensions were high between the two nations, and there was no doubt that the operation would be costly.

The role of Task Unit Whiskey in all of this was small but potentially critical. Noriega had plenty of places to hide and lots of ways to escape. One of these was a Panama Defense Forces (PDF) patrol boat, the *Presidente Porras*, and the SEAL task force was detailed to immobilize it.

A scout/swimmer from Naval Special Warfare Group One. His fashionable attire is essentially the same as that worn by the dive pairs attacking the Panamanian patrol boat: wet suit with hood and a Draeger rebreathing system (not scuba).

The mission was launched from Rodman Naval Station in Balboa Harbor, one of many US Navy installations in the Canal Zone. At 2300 hours, not quite two hours before the scheduled kickoff, the men slid into their wet suits, donned their closed-circuit breathing apparatus, and clambered into their big, black rubber inflatable boats. When the Combat Rubber Raiding Craft (CRRC) were loaded, the engines were started and the boats pushed off from shore, moving into the soft, inky night at minimum speed to avoid notice.

In the first boat, CRRC number 1, rode two combat swimmers, LT Edward Coughlin and EN3 Tim Eppley (dive pair number 1); CDR Norm Carley (the on-scene mission commander); HMC George Riley (coxswain); and HT3 Chris Kinney (machine gunner). CRRC number 2 carried a second dive pair, ET1 Randy Beausoleil and PH2 Chris Dye; remaining in the boat would be IS3 Scott Neudecker (coxswain), OS2 Mark Dodd (communicator), and QM3 Pat Malone (automatic weapons man).

Ashore, within the Rodman facility but still within range of the objective, a fire-support team manned .50-caliber heavy machine guns, Mk 19 automatic grenade launchers, and 60mm mortars, all preregistered on likely targets and equipped with night sights. Afloat, in case of trouble, two PBRs (Patrol Boat, River) carried more SEALs ready to intervene if the vulnerable "rubber ducks" were engaged by the PDF.

As seems to so often be the case, there was tremendous tension in the boats. Special forces like the SEALs are in the business of high-risk, high-payoff operations. They are expensive, in every respect, and to be successful everything has to be planned, rehearsed, scheduled, and orchestrated in mind-numbing detail. Deviations from the plan traditionally mean mission failure and often death for the people out on the pointy end of the spear. So, at precisely one hour before midnight, an hour and forty-five minutes before the bullets will fly all over Panama, Task Unit Whiskey's operation was already turning into what SEALs call a "goatscrew."

All the planning and the schedules had been based on a 2330 hours insertion time to reach and attack the target at 0100 (H-hour), but then the COMJSOTF (Commander Joint Special Operations Task Force) changed the insertion time to 2300 hours, adding to the stress level. But late in the planning sequence, just before the boats pushed off, Commander Carley was asked to push up his H-hour thirty minutes, to 0030. He refused; there wasn't enough time to get the swimmers to the target, arm the demolitions, and extract the swim teams with a thirty-minute advance in the schedule. The proposed change added another jolt of adrenaline to an already highly charged atmosphere.

Out in Balboa Harbor, the boats moved slowly and as silently as possible across the black water. There were bright lights ashore and boat traffic in the harbor, neither helping the SEALs with their stealthy approach to the point where the swimmers would slip over the gunwales and disappear on their mission. The outboards were not designed to run at such slow speeds; one began to run roughly and threatened to quit. But both boats made it to the shelter of a mangrove treeline on the north side of the harbor, across from Pier 18.

The SEALs waited and watched. Two

Hi ho, hi ho, it's off to work we go—with a Mk 138 satchel charge loaded with twenty pounds of water-resistant explosives, a dual priming system, and a pair of timers. The satchel charge is essentially iden- *tical to the old "mod zero" version of fifty years ago when the UDT swimmers cleared the beaches in Normandy and in the Pacific.*

boats moved across the harbor; was Noriega aboard? Were the Panamanians searching for US small boats or swimmers? The time for the boats to move out to the insertion point arrived. Boat number 1's engine fired up but boat number 2's refused to cooperate. Boat number 1 moved out alone while boat number 2, complete with frustrated boat crew and divers, stayed hidden in the mangroves.

In order to make up for the delays and still hit the required H-hour, the boat crew had to move a lot closer into the target than had been intended. At 2330 hours the first dive pair went over the side, into the water—on schedule. Commander Carley took boat number 1 back to the mangroves, took boat number 2 under tow, and got the second dive team out to the insertion point at 2335. Dive pair number 2 slipped over the side and disappeared.

After the swimmers departed, the SEALs were advised via radio that the H-hour for the whole show had been advanced fifteen minutes to 0045 local time, 20 December. This meant, of course, that the whole shooting match would kick off while the swimmers were at their objective and that their mission had suddenly become even more risky than anticipated. But there wasn't much to do except wait and watch and stay out of the way.

In the meantime, Commander Carley decided to take the boats back to Rodman and to change out the engine in CRRC number 2 with a spare. Boat number 2 was taken under tow again, and the little convoy slipped back across the water with practiced stealth. Two more Panamanian harbor craft transited Balboa Harbor; the SEALs evaded both and made it back to Rodman undetected and unscathed.

The dive pairs swam toward their objective about twenty feet below the surface. Instead of conventional scuba tanks, the swimmers wore Draeger rebreathing systems that recycle expelled air, clean it of carbon dioxide, then replenish it with oxygen. It is a closed system. No bubbles reached the surface to betray the swimmers' passage.

The swimmers had practiced for this mis-

A "rubber duck" is launched into the Pacific for some play time. The design is another bit of World War II surplus—a lifeboat that has been used for covert operations for half a century. It is simple, stable, reliable, cheap, stealthy, low-tech—just the ticket for special operators in US Special Operations Command.

sion for all their careers. For most it was their first-ever combat mission. Instead of employing some exotic, high-tech navigation system to find their way through the water, they used a system older than they were—determining their direction with a simple, luminous compass and measuring their distance by counting the number of kicks they made. It is a primitive system, decades old, that still works. After about half an hour underwater, dive pair number 2 (Beausoleil and Eppley) surfaced

Here's another simple, stealthy, low-tech piece of gear used in Panama: the compass board. Once trained and experienced in its use, a diver can navigate with precision below the surface, using the compass to maintain course and measuring distance traveled by counting kicks.

under Pier 18. It was a noisy place to be; a firefight began just as they arrived, visible to the fire-support teams ashore and to the boat teams. Who was firing at whom was unclear to the SEALs, and the mission proceeded as planned, despite underwater explosions in the area, probably from PDF personnel throwing hand grenades in the water to discourage just this kind of mission.

With the pier providing cover and concealment, Beausoleil and Eppley moved toward the target, still moored at its floating dock. They avoided swimming on the surface as they moved toward the patrol boat. At 0011 dive pair number 2 arrived at the *Presidente Porras,* positively identified it as the tar-

get, and executed the attack on the vessel. The two SEALs swam down under the stern, found the port propeller shaft, and began attaching and arming the explosive charge—just as they heard the engines of the ship start up.

The Mk 138 Mod 1 charge they'd carried through the dark water was a haversack loaded with twenty pounds of water-resistant explosive, complete with an MCS-1 clock, a Mk 39 safety and arming device, and a Mk 96 detonator, all designed to provide reliable delay and detonation of the main charge. In less than two minutes the charge was attached, armed, and ticking. Beausoleil and Eppley departed the target at 0013 hours, urged onward by explosions in the water nearby, and now made their way first to the shelter of nearby Pier 17, then to the extraction point where—they hoped—the boat would be waiting to pick them up.

A little late, dive pair number 1 arrived at 0014 and commenced their attack on the *Presidente Porras*. Despite the explosions and the firefight overhead, the SEALs moved along Pier 18 to the ship and installed their Mk 138 demolition system on the starboard propeller shaft. They tied a length of detonation cord from the haversack around the charge already in place on the port shaft, using a dual-priming technique to insure that both charges would detonate together for maximum effect.

At about 0017, after less than two minutes

at the target, Coughlin and Eppley removed the safeties and started the clock that would detonate the charges at 0100—if everything worked—and, as they say, got the hell out of Dodge. The PDF crews either knew or suspected what was going on and threw many grenades into the water, forcing the SEALs to the relative shelter of the pier pilings behind which they tried to avoid the effects of the nearby explosions. Finally they started to move away, but four more explosions sent shock waves through the water.

Because of the forty-five-minute delay on the charges and the enemy action in the vicinity of the target, both SEAL teams were trapped in the vicinity. They were still there

The first SEALs ashore are normally the scout/swimmer pair who precede the boat onto the beach, evaluate the threat level, then signal in the rubber duck with the rest of the crew. The wet suit is an important piece of gear, even for rough-tough SEALs—hypothermia is a problem for everybody.

A foundation for special operators from all services is the talent for popping up in the darndest places, unexpected and uninvited. This young lad looks a little waterlogged, as well he should because he and three teammates have been sitting on the bottom of San Diego Bay for an hour or so after navigating a few hundred meters below sailboats, water skiers, and the occasional recreational swimmer. He's been using a rebreather that recycles air, enriches it with oxygen, and emits no bubbles. The weapon is a Heckler & Koch MP4 9mm submachine gun, a favorite of special operators everywhere for urban and close combat.

at 0100 when the two Mk 138 demolition kits detonated as primed. While the swim pairs exited the target area, they noticed that all the PDF vessels in Balboa Harbor had started turning their propellers as an anti-swimmer defense.

The SEAL swimmers descended beneath the surface and swam out into the harbor on a course that brought them near the main shipping channel for vessels transiting the Panama Canal. In the grand tradition of military operations, yet another tactical problem presented itself now: a large, deep draft ship moving across the diver's intended course back to the extraction point. Although their Draegers were not designed for use at that depth, the swimmers descended to forty-five feet for ten minutes while the ship passed overhead, then ascended to the normal depth of twenty feet. At last they found the shelter of Pier 6 and from there proceeded to the pickup point at the end of the pier for extraction.

The two CRRCs were waiting. In fact, they'd been waiting for what had seemed an eternity, since about 0055. The dive pairs were extremely late for their planned extraction. The boat crews, the support teams, and the fire-support teams ashore had all seen the firefight in the vicinity of the target; they'd seen the charges go off on schedule. They'd endured a firefight of their own in the immediate vicinity of the extraction point, near Pier 6, where they'd held their fire while tracers zipped overhead, apparently at random. They'd monitored their radios, without word from the teams whose own waterproofed MX-300s had been unequal to the task of communicating with the support elements.

Commander Carley, worried that the dive pairs may have mistaken an adjacent pier for the extraction point, sent CRRC number 2 over to investigate, hoping that the swimmers were there; they weren't and the boat was recalled.

An hour later than planned, at 0200 hours, dive pair number 1 materialized from the gloom, much to the relief of the boat crews. About five minutes later the second group showed up, too, intact. The four SEALs were hauled back aboard the rubber boats, and the teams executed a tactical withdrawal. Using infrared strobes as a preplanned recognition device, the boats returned to the relative safety of Rodman at 0220 hours. An hour and a half later, Task Unit Whiskey was declared ready for retasking.

Mission Overview

Task Unit Whiskey's little adventure in Balboa Harbor is a kind of classic in the SEAL bag of tricks, revealing the hazards and virtues of naval special operations. Naval Special Warfare (NSW), as it is called, has been a very important and much abused subject for the last fifty years. For the US Navy it goes back to the Underwater Demolition Teams of World War II, who cleared beach obstacles and surveyed gradients for amphibious landings in the Pacific and against European shores, many dying in the attempt. It is an extremely dangerous set of missions that cannot be practically executed with other, less demanding means.

The organization and the people of the Naval Special Warfare is actually two communities, one being the men in the water, the Sea/Air/Land "commandos" (or SEALs), and the other being the men on the water, the Special Boat Squadrons (SBS). Both have a long and distinguished combat record, and both

It can be a long, cold swim back to base, so when the bus stops to pick up the team there's always a scramble to get aboard. Here, a cargo net has been rigged off the bow to make recovery of the people in the water a bit more expeditious. The Naval Special Warfare community is well represented here, the guys in the water (SEALs) and the guys on water (Special Boat Squadron members).

Membership in the SEALs is not for everyone. It requires tremendous toughness—some physical, most mental. While this healthy specimen looks as though he may have previously worked for a professional football team, most SEALs are of normal size and stature. These people are accepted into membership in a tiny community (about 1,200 men total) only after a long, rigorous process of testing, evaluation, and selection—more than actual training. Anyone can learn the technical skills required to do the things SEALs do, but few have the personal self-discipline to learn the internal, intangible skills needed to be a good operator.

communities have been linked together as Naval Special Warfare for about thirty years. While the SEALs get most of the attention and notoriety, the SBS have been doing a lot of the shooting and bleeding over the years. While most of the SBS crews are not graduates of the Basic Underwater Demolition /SEALS (BUD/S) training program the boat officers are SEALs, and SBS personnel are held

to the same high standard of performance as the more notorious part of the team. This story is about both.

The men in Naval Special Warfare are just one part of a big, broad spectrum of American combat power—in fact, a tiny slice of the pie. There are only about 1,500 of them in the US Navy, far fewer than the US Army's 7,000 or so Green Berets (active and reserve). SEALs, along with the Army's Ranger regiment and Special Forces groups, comprise the United States most elite surface combat operations resources. All are masters of basic infantry tactics; each has its own area of expertise. All train together at some points of their qualification. All, despite their parentage as components of the Navy or Army, are really on-call assets for the highest levels of the National Command Authority (NCA)—the president, the secretary of defense, and the Joint Chiefs of Staff. When they go to war, their mission will probably start at MacDill Air Force Base, Florida, where the United States Special Operations Command (USSOCOM) is headquartered. It is that kind of organization: powerful, dangerous, expensive, and above all, *special*. There is also something traditionally a bit odd about these special forces soldiers and sailors. They are isolated and aloof from the rest of the military and especially from the public, partly by design and partly by tradition. So how and why do a book like this one?

This book is the result of a policy of the US Department of Defense and the Navy to release as much information as possible about military institutions and activities while maintaining operational security. That can be a tough compromise sometimes, particularly with communities in special operations. In this case, it means that this book is the product of a close collaboration with the Navy, with the SEAL community, and with individual SEALs. All the photography of active-duty SEALs in this book has been reviewed and approved by both US Naval Special Warfare Command (SPECWARCOM) and SEAL Teams Three and Five, who assisted with its production.

The Big Picture: US Special Operations Command

Special Operations Command has become, in the years since the failed Iranian hostage rescue mission, one of the best funded, most secure, most competitive parts of the US force structure. All the services, including the Coast Guard, have been caught up to some extent in the reorientation away from what is called "high-intensity combat," with its need for nuclear weapons, long-range bombers, numerous tank divisions and aircraft carriers, to preparation for "low-intensity combat," the work of small teams of extremely adept people like SEALs and Green Berets.

USSOCOM is just one of eight "unified" commands within the US armed forces and has been a major player in the defenses of America since 1987. It integrates assets from all the services into one organization, with one commander, and with the same basic set of missions for everybody. That doesn't mean that everybody does the same thing; rather it means that the Navy, Army, and Air Force pool their talents and resources for planning, training, and executing missions.

Special operations forces have traditionally been the "bad boys" of all the services. Many senior officers have, over the years, been candid about their loathing of the "cowboys" within their large, conservative organizations. Special forces training and missions produce a kind of lunatic intensity that is accepted within these groups but that clashes badly with the larger Navy or Army community within which it is supposed to function. Special operators have a reputation (well earned by an earlier generation) of using their own, independent criteria for acceptable behavior. Green Berets used to say, when asked if they were in the Army, "No, I'm in Special Forces." Some still do.

Becoming a SEAL or a Green Beret has never, as a result, been considered the fast track to high rank. It was, and still is, a special place for special men (and, very rarely and not in the SEALs, a few incredible women) who consider these extremely demanding roles

Naval Special Warfare is an interesting blend of high technology and the most basic, simple warrior skills. This fire team, coming ashore in a practiced ritual, functions much as small units have for thousands of years—with the same kinds of missions, the same concerns, discomforts, stresses. Norsemen invading England must, with minor changes in equipment and uniform, have looked like this.

a kind of calling. They aren't in the business to get rich or famous but to be measured by the highest standard of military performance and found acceptable. That is the real lure and the real reward of the special forces.

While the special operators may not always be personally popular within their services, the additional stress and funding for such missions has made for a very competitive budgetary environment. Both the Army and the Marine Corps compete with the Navy for the missions done by the SEALs. In fact, you could stand on a beach being infiltrated by combat swimmers and be very hard pressed to

17

There is tremendous overlap of missions, training, aptitude, and command of all the organizations within US Special Operations Command. This Green Beret trains SEALs in the art and science of small arms like the German GPMG 7.62mm ma-chine gun he's carrying. SEALs and Green Berets are essentially members of the same fraternity. They are likely to be on better terms with each other than with members of conventional units within their own branch of service.

know who was about to kill you—American Army "Green Berets" or Rangers, Marine Corps Force Recon, or US Navy SEALs. All use precisely the same weapons, boats, dive gear, radios, and uniforms—and all train for what sometimes looks like the same exact mission. But it turns out that the missions are not quite exact, that there are distinctions, and that the overlap is not as great as it initially appears. Here, then, is a thumbnail description of how the confusing world of US Special Operations is split up and tied together.

JSOC

Joint Special Operations Command (JSOC) is a kind of planning and coordination cell, headquartered at Pope Air Force Base, North Carolina, (co-located with Fort Bragg). JSOC's primary mission is to study the techniques and requirements of all the Special Operation Forces (SOF) components, including Naval Special Warfare, to ensure that—as they say—everybody's playing off the same sheet of music.

USASOC

The Army contributes the "Green Berets" (properly but rarely called Special Forces), a

SEALs now have a hostage rescue/counterterrorist assignment to train for. These SEALs are training for it by being "proned-out" by some Marines during a training exercise aboard the USNS Joshua Humphries in the Red Sea. This kind of joint training is a standard feature of life in the teams.

regiment of Rangers, the Delta counterterrorist unit, a special operations aviation unit called Task Force 160 (TF-160), plus psychological, civil affairs, and signal units. Most of these units are headquartered at Fort Bragg, North Carolina, at the US Army Special Operations Command (USASOC).

AFSOC

The Air Force contribution to special warfare is the US Air Force Special Operations Command (AFSOC) with headquarters at Hurlburt Field, Florida. The Air Force provides special aircraft and crews to insert and extract Army and Navy combat elements and to support them from overhead. AFSOC owns and operates special versions of the C-130, CH-53, and CH-60 within the 1st Special Operations Wing.

NAVSOC

The Navy's contribution to USSOCOM is called NAVSOC within the special operations community, but is in fact Naval Special Warfare Command—SEALs and Special Boat Squadrons.

SEAL Specialties

SEALs—by contrast with Air Force and Army special operators in the Ranger regiment and special forces groups—are generalists, although each will have a specialty (intelligence, submarine operations, weapons, engineering, communications), that he does in support of the organization in the planning process. But once the little squad of SEALs goes off to war, he has to be able to do the job of anybody else on the team. "If I'm the platoon commander on a mission and I take a hit," one SEAL officer says, "the assistant platoon commander can take over. It doesn't matter if he was the corpsman or the radioman— he can take over that operation and direct it to completion. I can pick up the radio, treat a wound, use any of the weapons. Green Berets say they can do that too, but I think we build *generalists* while they build *specialists*. That's probably because they operate in larger groups. We operate in groups anywhere from four to sixteen men, and any one of our guys can slip into the role of any other guy . . . within limitations."

SEAL Missions

Just about all the special operations forces have the same *basic* list of missions. Each of them adapts these missions to the unique talents of the force. For the NSW community the list looks like this:

1) Direct action (DA)—Short-term seize, destroy, damage, or capture operations. Attacks against facilities ashore or afloat; "prisoner snatch" operations; small offensive combat operations against hostile forces.

2) Special reconnaissance (SR)—Reconnaissance and surveillance operations. Covert beach surveys, listening posts, observation posts.

3) Unconventional warfare (UW)—training, leading, and equipping partisan and guer-

The Air Force contribution to Special Operations Command is two-fold: it offers a kind of bus service, like this SH-60 dropping a squad off in the Gulf, *complete with boat; and it provides a kind of bodyguard service overhead, with Spectre gunships.*

rilla forces, behind enemy lines.

4) Foreign internal defense (FID)—Training, advising, and teaching the military, paramilitary, and law enforcement personnel of allied nations. Professional development, normally in a noncombat environment.

5) Counterterrorist operations (CT)—Operations conducted against terrorist units and individuals. May be as direct responses to terrorist operations or as indirect, preventive, deterrence measures.

All these missions have implications for their missionaries. To accomplish missions like these and survive, the people and the organizations they belong to need to be agile (individually and organizationally), trained to a far higher standard than conventional military personnel, and provided with far more resources, man for man, than conventional units. This assignment makes for organizations that are expensive and exclusive.

The "Wiring Diagram"

SPECWARCOM is an interesting community and a tremendous challenge to command. Although the SEAL teams are its most famous component, they are only one part of the whole business of Naval Special Warfare—a fairly small part, in fact.

RADM Ray Smith commands two major combat resources, Special Warfare Group One and Two. Each of these groups include three SEAL teams, a Special Boat Squadron, and a Swimmer Delivery Vehicle team.

Group One operates out of Coronado, California, and generally deploys forces to the Pacific and the Persian Gulf; SEAL teams One, Three, and Five are assigned to Group One. Group Two is headquartered at Little Creek, Virginia, with teams Two, Four, and Eight assigned, and a responsibility for operations in and around the Atlantic, including Europe and Latin America. These two headquarters are the administrative foundations for special warfare and, despite the sneers from the operators in the field about the "puzzle palace" (as such headquarters are often called) they are essential for the efficient coordination of as-

The fundamental component of the SEALs is the dive pair. A cardinal rule of life in the teams is you never abandon your swim buddy. It is too dangerous a business for solo operators.

sets and activities.

Coronado is not only home to Naval Special Warfare and Group One, but also to the notorious Naval Special Warfare Center where SEALs are trained. Basic Underwater Demolition/SEAL training is conducted at Coronado, the entry point for all new SEALs and SEAL Delivery Team members. The center also conducts advanced training and professional development programs for members of the SPECWARCOM community.

Little Creek, besides hosting Group Two, is responsible for the Special Warfare Development Group. This is the SEAL think tank

where new weapons, tactics, communication systems, and dive equipment is tested, evaluated, and written into doctrine. Little Creek is also responsible for the development of special operations tactics for air, ground, and maritime forces, in and out of Naval Special Warfare. SPECWARCOM includes detachments in Alaska and Hawaii, plus five Special Warfare Units.

What you don't see advertised are the semi-covert programs called Development Group and Red Cell. Development Group provides support for a variety of classified programs that—sorry—we aren't going to tell you about. Red Cell is an offshoot from the Naval Security Coordination Team and has the interesting mission of assisting navy commands around the world with their security problems. This help is not always welcomed because it is done in a sneaky way when the Red Cell members sneak or break into what are supposed to be secure facilities. They are supposed to act like terrorists or subversives—and that's the way a lot of people outside Naval Special Warfare think of them, too. Some commanders seem to think Red Cell creates more security problems than it solves. This program was at one time extremely notorious and the subject of a book by one of its former commanders (written while in prison) that scandalized Naval Special Warfare generally. It appears at this writing that the program will be transferred out of NSW into the more conventional Naval Investigative Service.

SEAL and Special Boat Squadron Basics

Although we usually refer to this community as SEALs, it is a bigger, more complicated business than the SEALs alone. The other

This fire team represents half a squad, a quarter of a platoon. Units this size are perfectly suited to most SEAL ops—ideal for ambushes, for example, and many strike missions. The fire team is small enough to be fast and agile and almost invisible; it is big enough to provide mutual support and to have enough diversity and cargo capacity to go inland for a raid or a recon.

23

SEALs get considerable latitude in the kind of gear and weapons they carry and use. This officer's non-standard combat vest is based on a design concept developed by the Israelis and adopted by the British, along with some US Special Operations Forces personnel. Rifle magazines are stowed in pouches designed for easy access—and to provide some protection against enemy small arms fire and grenade fragments.

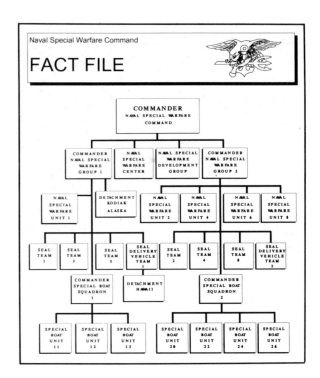

Naval Special Warfare Command

FACT FILE

This is the "wiring diagram" for Naval Special Warfare—minus the "black" programs and units. Essentially it shows two major communities, Group One for the Pacific and Group Two for the Atlantic. The units are forward-deployment bases. Not shown are Red Cell and Development Group.

major part of SPECWARCOM is the guys on the surface who go through the same training at BUD/S, go off on the same missions, and bleed at least as much as the members of the SEAL teams—the Special Boat Squadrons and the members of the Special Warfare Units. They're all Naval Special Warfare members, although all the attention and glory seems to go to the SEALs alone. But, as the history of Naval Special Warfare in Vietnam and after shows, much of the combat and the killing has been done by the riverine warriors duking it out with the bad guys ashore with .50-caliber machine guns and Mk 19 grenade launchers, all while roaring around in their PBRs in an unstealthy way.

The idea behind the boat squadrons is to provide the SEAL teams with dedicated, "organic" mobility, as well as some kinds of special patrol and surface strike missions. These squadrons are commanded by SEALs but manned largely by sailors from the surface warfare community, what SEALs often call the "black shoe" navy. Although part of the Naval Special Warfare community, they are not quite SEALs but SEAL support units.

The home base for SEAL/SBS operations seems somehow out of place on the luxurious, tropical paradise of Coronado, California, just

Far from the water but cold anyway, these two SEALs are participating in a training exercise in Norway. Special operators have to be extremely versatile and tolerant of extremes.

across the bay from San Diego. While tanned tourists frolic on the beach nearby, SEAL/SBS operations and training are planned and conducted at the Naval Special Warfare Command (SPECWARCOM), a component of US Special Warfare Command. The headquarters is just another rather modern concrete building, complete with the requisite lawn and landscaping, plus plenty of chain-link fence, guards, and razor wire.

The US Navy takes the prize for inventing and actually using the world's biggest and most awkward acronyms, one of which is SPECWARCOM. You might as well get used to words like this because everybody in the SEAL/SBS community uses them all the time; they are unavoidable. SPECWARCOM is the parent headquarters for all Navy special operations of which SEALs are only a part.

The commander of SPECWARCOM currently is a lean, bouncy, cheery, young-looking man with a star on his collar: he's Vice Admiral Ray Smith, fifty years old, who's been part of the community since 1970. Like all American commanders, he will have custody of SPECWARCOM for two or three years, then hand it over to a new boss. During those years he will be responsible for the health and wealth of the community, its training, its tactics, its fitness for combat. He, like his predecessors and successors, will try to guide SPECWARCOM through the hazards of annual budgets and Department of Defense policy changes.

SEAL Teams

On paper at least, a full-up SEAL team includes ten platoons of SEALs plus a small support staff from the black-shoe navy. This support staff are the yeomen for administrative support, radiomen, ordnance specialists, a navy diver to help with the dive locker—about twenty non-SEAL personnel. There is an additional command element including the commanding officer, executive officer, and operations officer, all of whom are fully SEAL-qualified.

While in theory there are ten platoons in each team, it doesn't usually work out that neatly. Each team has an intense training program that cuts into the number of people actually available to participate in a platoon. But each of the platoons will have sixteen SEALs assigned: two officers and fourteen enlisted members. These are grouped further into two squads of eight, each getting an officer and seven enlisted. The squads themselves are split into fire teams of four men, the fire teams each having two "swim pairs."

The squad has traditionally been the organization of choice for SEAL operations and has turned out to be a very efficient group for many missions.

A lot of SEAL equipment is designed around these groups. The Mk V patrol boat is designed to accommodate sixteen SEALs. Fire teams of four fully combat-loaded SEALs fit very nicely into a Combat Rubber Raiding Craft. The Patrol Craft, Mk 1 is designed to carry a squad of eight SEALs.

SEAL Mobile Training Teams

SEALs (and Green Berets, too) are deployed all over the world, all the time, on quiet little assignments that you never read about in the papers—even when dramatic things happen, and the proverbial poop hits that fabled propeller. These deployments have a couple of functions: one is to put the special forces people out near the scene of a possible crime, before it is committed, ready to respond; the other is to train in environments a lot more realistic than are available in the United States.

One of these quiet deployments ("dets" in the trade jargon) nobody ever hears about is in support of the anti-drug war in Central and South America. Although US law prohibits SEAL/SBSs and other American military personnel from active combat, US policy is to use special operations forces personnel to train the "trigger pullers" to a high standard. And executing that mission is the team of Naval Special Warfare Unit Eight (NSWU-8) and Special Boat Squadron Twenty-Six (SBS-26), forward based out of Rodman in Panama but with people and boats busy in many Latin American nations.

These organizations, along with SEAL Team Four, are tasked with providing Mobile Training Teams (MTTs) to Bolivia, Argentina, Brazil, Colombia, Equador, and other nations where drugs are manufactured. All these countries have extensive river systems; there are more than 140,000 miles of navigable rivers in South America, with 20,000 in Bolivia alone. These become the highways for transportation of drugs. To control the drug flow requires efficient, effective patrol of the rivers, something the Special Boat Squadron folks do better than anybody.

The MTTs involve quite small numbers of US personnel and equipment to train rather large numbers of host-nation personnel. Sometimes the SBS/SEAL team doesn't even supply the boats. Once on scene the SBS team starts working with the boat operators from the host nation while the SEALs work with the police or military people who will do the patrolling ashore. In Bolivia this force is called the "Blue Devils"; it has been almost entirely trained by these MTTs. The SBS and SEAL dets have helped the Bolivians develop four bases for counterdrug operations deep in the jungle.

In Colombia the story is a little different. The US Marine Corps runs the show there,

Although the basic uniform matches that of Army and some Navy units, the CAR-15 version of the M16 is pretty much unique to the special operators. The CAR-15 has a shorter barrel and a collapsible buttstock.

Special operators place a high premium on surprise, stealth, and speed. A lot of all three come from the SBS crews and their exotic little boats, like this 30-foot rigid inflatable boat (RIB) seen here zipping around with a fire team of SEALs embarked.

Deep recon and strike missions are usually the province of the Army's Rangers or Green Berets, but SEALs train hard to do the same thing. Who will get the call for one of these assignments will have a lot to do with who is closest to the scene of the crime, *rather than any particular special talent. All are good, but if the op happens to be a coastal target it may be a platoon or squad of SEALs who "take it down."*

where they've had a long and chummy relationship with the Colombian marines. The Colombian det includes one officer and four enlisted SBS/SEAL personnel, all with a special interest in riverine operations and with Spanish language skills. MTTs in Colombia, as elsewhere in the program, last six months.

Special Warfare Units and Forward Basing

Since there are so few SEALs to go around, and since the "real world" has a way of blowing up in your face unexpectedly, Naval Special Warfare has developed forward bases closer to the potential hot spots of the world

than Coronado or Little Creek. These are the Naval Special Warfare Units (NSWUs), each with people, facilities, and equipment intended to speed up the process of planning and launching missions.

There are five NSWUs. When the "real world" starts acting up these are reorganized as Naval Special Warfare Task Groups and Units and start manning up with extra personnel from in and out of the NSW community. An emergency will probably find assets getting requisitioned from other NSWUs, particularly the exotic, complex Swimmer Delivery Vehicle (SDV), which may be flown in from the US.

Two SWUs serve the European Command area from bases in Spain and Scotland. The Naval Special Warfare Unit base in Spain (NSWU-6) uses Rigid Inflatable Boats (RIBs), Patrol Coastal boats (PCs), and Mk V patrol boats. The base in Scotland (NSWU-2) uses RIBs only. The Pacific Command is served by NSWU-1, recently repositioned from the Philippines to Guam; like NSWU-6, it uses RIBs, PCs, and Mk V patrol boats. NSWU-8 serves the extremely busy Southern Command out of Rodman Naval Station in Panama, supporting the busy counternarcotics operations with a mix of riverine and coastal patrol boats and the RIBs. Detachments in Hawaii and Alaska provide SEALs with a broad range of training options.

Besides these forward bases, two large Naval Special Warfare Groups on the east and west coasts of the US provide a continental United States (CONUS) foundation for operations "downrange."

For some Naval Special Warfare assets, forward basing is the only practical way to show up on time for the little "come as you are" wars that are the stock in trade of US Special Operations Forces. The PCs, for example, are far too big to go anywhere except under their own power. Although they are fast, it's a mighty big world. If they had to self-deploy from the US, it could take these ships almost three weeks to arrive at some possible operational areas.

Change of Mission

The "commander's intent" for American special operations has changed quite a bit since the idea was first used fifty years ago, at the outset of World War II. Back then the idea was to provide support for partisans and guerrillas in occupied France, Yugoslavia, China, and elsewhere. It involved very little—if any—direct combat. It was a training, leading, and supplying role for forces that tried their best to avoid direct contact with German or Japanese forces while collecting intelligence and sabotaging vehicles, railroads, and bridges and occasionally assassinating individual enemy.

Special Operations Forces today still train for that mission, and SEALs execute something like it every day, in nations all over the world. The trainees aren't guerrillas anymore, but soldiers, sailors, and law enforcement officers from nations such as Colombia, Bolivia, and Kuwait; and the "enemy" is now quite often the guerrilla-like forces who manufacture and distribute drugs or terrorists in Ireland, the Middle East, or Latin America.

The war against terrorist forces has, more than anything else, inspired much of the mission of today's SEALs and other SOF commu-

This lieutenant commands a SEAL Team Three platoon conducting training in desert patrolling, small unit tactics, and live-fire exercises. Unlike many other units, particularly conventional ones, SEALs train their officers and enlisted people together at the same time. While it puts additional stresses on the officers, who must fulfill administrative duties as well as survive the program, it has the advantage of applying the same high standards to the commissioned officers, while their followers observe. The result is an extra measure of respect for a SEAL officer.

"Takedown" missions are complicated, dangerous raids that require tremendous skill to execute. When they go bad, they go real bad; the consequences aren't just death or embarrassment for the team, but possible dire international ramifications as well. Ever since the failed Iranian hostage rescue, this mission has been practiced over and over, in depth and detail.

Although SEALs try to avoid airborne insertions like this (as one team commander says, "If you have to jump—find another way!"), the technique is still used occasionally and is practiced as just one way of getting from here to there.

nities. The tasking for Naval Special Warfare is now, essentially, to be prepared to *conduct short-notice small-unit operations at night, over the horizon, to infiltrate from sea, air or land, in adverse weather.* Instead of training others to fight large, conventional battles, SOF units, including the SEALs, are much more like global SWAT teams that can be sent to fight almost anybody, almost anywhere. Like a good SWAT team, these forces are task-organized and are based on stealth, shock, surprise, and precision. While some SEALs still study foreign languages and are charismatic instructors for people of extremely alien cultures, the heavy emphasis now is on preparing SEALs to be able to slither deep into hostile territory, up to easy pistol range of

very specific bad guys, put 9mm bullets between their eyes—and then get out without being obvious about it. The battlefield can be a hotel, an airliner, a civilian cargo ship, an oil platform, a factory, or an embassy. And the enemy may be one hostile man—or woman—surrounded by innocents.

This is a tall order. In fact, it is sometimes too tall; SEALs aren't, despite what you hear, supermen. They get tapped to do impossible missions sometimes because they are so skilled, so sneaky, so confident . . . and they die in the attempt, sometimes, as in Panama and Grenada, when they're pushed beyond their limits. There are only about 1,200 of them for a global set of responsibilities. It is a small community with a huge mission.

This motley crew is a squad of warrior SEALs from long ago and far away. Standing are Pierre Birtz, Bill Garnett, Charlie Bump, and Bob Gormly; kneeling are Jess Tollison and Fred McCarty; the photo was made in 1967. With Gormly (then a lieutenant) as squad leader, these men operated around the town of Binh Thuy, helping establish the reputation of the SEALs as among the most elite American warriors. All made Naval Special Warfare a profession, and all are now retired except for Tollison, who was killed in an accident at the Niland, California, training facility in 1971. Gormly went on to command SEAL Teams Two and Six, UDT-12, and NSW Group Two before retiring in 1992 as a captain. Bob Gormly collection

Chapter 2

A Short History Lesson

The keel for today's SEALs and Special Boat Squadrons was laid in May of 1942 with the formation of the Naval Combat Demolition Unit at Fort Pierce, Florida. The men who were selected for the program came from the Naval Construction Battalions and the Navy/Marine Corps Scout and Raider Volunteers. All had extensive swim experience; some were commercial divers; all were in superb physical condition. The training was not too different, fifty years ago, from today—lots of physical training (PT), lots of swimming, lots of demolitions. The stress level was high, by design. Training continued day and night, in the swamps with the alligators, on the beaches, and offshore.

The motivation for the program had come toward the end of the previous year. After less than a year of war, the United States was beginning to strike back at the entrenched Japanese, first at Guadalcanal, then, in November, at Tarawa . . . "terrible Tarawa," as it will always be known to the United States Marine Corps.

The US was badly unprepared for war, and even more unprepared for large-scale, long-range amphibious operations. One of the things that makes wars interesting is the ways in which individuals and nations respond to the surprises and stresses imposed on them by events. In the case of the US Navy and Marine Corps in 1942, this meant a re-

quirement for not merely the attack of Japanese installations in the Pacific, but the seizure of critical bases.

Guadalcanal came first—and the invasion phase of the operation, at least, was a cakewalk. The Marines were able to step ashore, essentially unopposed, often with dry feet. Getting the force ashore was just about the least of the problems at Guadalcanal—most of which came soon thereafter. The Navy had been lucky with that phase of the operation. Tarawa was different. D-day for Tarawa was 20 November 1942. Information about the island, its defenses, and its approaches was limited. Hydrographic data was sketchy, tidal data almost nonexistent. The assault force commander took a risk, knowing the stakes, and lost.

The Marines were sent in aboard conventional landing craft. Five hundred yards offshore, within the range of Japanese machine guns, the boats ground to a halt against coral reefs. The Marines, in the grand tradition, jumped off the boat ramps for the long wade into the beach . . . and died in droves. Many stepped into depressions in the coral reef; heavily loaded, they sank and drowned. The rest had to endure the heavy, interlocking fields of fire from the Japanese defenders. It was a disaster.

Hundreds of Marines died before the battle for Tarawa really even began. In a way,

Many of the basic "frogman" techniques in use today were invented half a century ago in the pressure cooker of war. That includes this technique for deploying a line of swimmers off an enemy-held beach from a high-speed boat.

their lives were wasted, but in another way, by dying this way, they taught the Navy a lesson. The lesson was, and still is, that amphibious assaults are high-risk operations that require careful preparation. And that need for battlefield preparation was the idea for the development of the Navy Combat Demolition Unit.

Their mission was to scout possible invasion beaches and to clear, with explosives, obstacles that might prevent the invasion force from reaching the beach as had happened at

Tarawa. It was recognized that there were essentially four hazards to the force: enemy action from fortifications ashore, enemy-built obstacles such as concrete blocks placed in the water, natural obstacles such as the coral reef that stopped the Marines, and the time and range of the tides.

That was the program for the sturdy volunteers at Fort Pierce. The survivors of the challenging training were organized as small units, structured with six enlisted men and one officer per Combat Demolition Unit and shipped off to England with the rest of the American contingent building up for the invasion of France.

When finally, on 6 June 1944, Allied forces were ready to take Europe back from the Nazis, the first men ashore were the Navy Combat Demolition Teams (NCDTs). The NCDT members were tasked with the nasty chore of surveying and destroying the beach obstacles emplaced by the Germans along the Normandy coast of France. These obstacles were an ingenious and extensive array of concrete blocks, steel spikes, mines, and barbed wire that cluttered most of the beaches suitable for amphibious landings. Left in place, they certainly would deter any large force from putting men ashore. And in 1943 the Germans knew the Allies were going to come, sooner or later, and were working as fast as possible to make a beach passage as costly as possible.

When the Allies finally struck, the NCDT men were out in front of the first wave. With the most primitive equipment, utterly lacking effective protection from the chilly water, they swam in to the beach in the small hours before the invasion. Working from one massive obstacle to the next, hanging satchel charges linked with detonation cord, they prepared to clear the beaches for the assault elements.

Dawn that day found an incredible armada off the Normandy coast, thousands of ships and boats finally bringing hundreds of thousands of soldiers back to Europe—and the beaches still hadn't been completely cleared. The NCDT men had been given a tall order, and not all the obstacles had been blown by the time the infantry started in to the beach. As the cloudy sky brightened, German gunners could see, and engage, the men setting charges on the beach whose mission was obvious. While the NCDT men struggled frantically to avoid the fire, emplace the explosives, and blow the lanes for the landing craft, the first wave closed on the beaches.

Even without clear access to some of the beaches, the craft disgorged their cargoes of infantry when and where they could, often under intense artillery and heavy machine gun fire. The NCDT men worked as fast as they could, but even so they found infantry sheltering behind obstacles rigged and primed for demolition, despite warning devices. Some charges blew with infantry nearby, killing them, while other obstacles weren't blown because of the proximity of men from the first wave.

Even so, four lanes were cleared and the assault elements generally made it ashore—if not in good order, at least in one piece, one infantry division after another. The cost for the NCDT force was far higher than for the infantry—about thirty percent at Utah Beach, about sixty-five percent at Omaha, about forty percent casualties overall. But, from the point

February, 1969. A SEAL ties a block of C4 into a line of det cord before placing the charge in a Viet Cong (VC) tunnel complex. Vietnam honed the special warfare abilities of the little SEAL community to a sharp edge through an emphasis on small unit, independent operations that made individual platoons and squads responsible for "taking care of business."

of view of the planners, that was a small price to pay for getting a secure foothold on the heavily defended enemy shore.

Despite the losses and the problems the NCDT units encountered, their work was considered a success and adapted to the island-hopping campaign in the Pacific. They were rechristened Underwater Demolition Teams (UDT), each with 100 enlisted men and thirteen officers assigned, and retaining the seven-man unit foundation.

Out in the Pacific the UDT units developed a routine that became part of the standard operating procedure (SOP) for amphibious assaults, some of which survives to the present day. This routine started with a beach reconnaissance four days before the scheduled assault (D-minus-4) with the swimmers inserted just at first or last light. This recon would identify obstacles, natural and man-made, on the intended lanes for the landing craft and armored amphibious tractors (AAM-TRACs), recording each carefully and developing a chart of the offshore, nearshore, foreshore, backshore, and hinterland areas of the invasion beaches.

On D-minus-1 or on D-day itself the obstacles would be blown. The method developed fifty years ago is still taught today because it still works. Here's how they did it:

While naval gunfire and close air support aircraft light up the beach with guns, bombs, rockets, and cannon fire in this type of approach, a small, fast ship makes a high-speed run into the beach. During World War II, modified destroyer-escorts were used and designated APDs (Attack Personnel Destroyers). Several miles offshore the APD stopped and lowered four LCPR landing craft, each with a "rubber duck" lashed to the port side. These LCPRs then made a high-speed "splash run" parallel to the beach, about a thousand meters out, starboard side facing the shore. One after another the swimmers rolled out of the LCPR into the rubber duck and, on command, into the water, forming a line of swimmers. At a thousand meters the small portion of each man's head is essentially invisible, and while

the defenders might possibly have spotted one with powerful binoculars, the aerial bombardment and naval gunfire tended to make them worry about other issues.

The men swam ashore and executed their missions, either a reconnaissance or a beach clearance, then withdrew back to the thousand-meter line offshore for pickup, again forming a line of swimmers at intervals. The LCPR came zooming up the line again, with a rubber sling extended. By forming a crook with his right arm and kicking hard just before the boat came by, the swimmer could come up partially out of the water and snag the sling rigged from the inflatable boat, to then be smoothly plucked from the ocean slingshot fashion. One after another the line of swimmers could be quickly and (under the circumstances) safely recovered.

The actual demolition of the beach obstacles also became something of an art form, still practiced today. That technique sent swimmers in to assigned obstacles with satchel charges essentially identical to the ones used today. The flank swimmers at either end of the line carried long rolls of "det cord" instead of explosives; while the other swimmers were busy installing the satchel charges, the det cord was strung from one end of the beach to the other. The satchel charges were each tied into this det cord, and then most of the swimmers began to withdraw. Finally, the ends of the det cord were double-primed, once from each end, with a blasting cap and time fuse. Using waterproof fuse lighters, the fuse was lit, and the whole team formed up out at the thousand-meter line for pickup. When either of the fuses finally burned down to its blasting cap, the "powder train" was initiated; the det cord linked all the charges and caused all to go off within a small fraction of a second—hopefully while the swimmers were already well offshore and safe from the blast effect and chunks of concrete and steel that rained down after such a mission. After Normandy, UDT losses dropped to only about one percent from the approximately forty percent of the first large-scale operation, thanks large-

"Hey! You said the mud wasn't deep!" The op hasn't even started and this guy is already out of action— up to his knees in mud. The weapon is the infamous Stoner, a 5.56mm machine gun with a tendency to jam at embarrassing moments. When it worked, though, it could chew up whatever it was pointed at, and the idea behind it survives today in the light-weight version of the M60 still used by the squads.

ly to this technique. By the end of the war thirty-four teams, including about 3,500 officers and men, were in action in the Pacific.

Korea

In the grand American military tradition, much of the equipment and experience of the UDTs in World War II was discarded promptly after VJ-day—only to be reinvented a few years later. For UDT that came in September 1950 with the audacious amphibious landing at Inchon, Korea.

With United Nations (UN) forces trapped in a shrinking perimeter at the southern tip of

Korea by a rampaging, nearly victorious North Korean army, Gen. Douglas MacArthur and his staff designed an "end run" operation on the enemy, with the port city of Inchon on the western coast of the peninsula, near the already fallen capital of Seoul, as the target.

The harbor at Inchon is a treacherous one, with an extreme range of tides that would make the timing and execution of any amphibious operation extremely critical. To minimize the danger, UDT was used to provide detailed information about channels, docks, tides, and defenses. They cleared channels of mines the hard way, by hand, swimming in line-abreast and attaching charges to the mines as they were encountered.

After the Inchon invasion totally changed the complexion of the war, with the North Koreans reeling back, the UDT units were used again, but not just for beach recons and clearance missions. Their skill and experience earned them assignments to blow bridges, railroads, tunnels, and similar targets well away from the beaches.

Korea was the first of a series of nasty little wars that didn't conform to the expectations of the strategic planners in Washington, but that didn't prevent soldiers, sailors, and Marines from having to fight them. Korea didn't really fit what the American public expected, either, and consequently support for the war and the men fighting it slowly ebbed a bit until the stalemate was formalized with a truce in 1953. But Korea expanded the mission of the organization that would soon be rechristened "SEALs" and included guerrilla operations behind the lines, parachute jumps, and other missions quite different from those envisioned ten years previously during the bigger conflict of World War II. And more was yet to come.

The Vietnam War

Although the ancestors of the units and the missions that would become the Navy's and Army's special operations forces existed during World War II, it was not until 1962 that they achieved real recognition and support. The support came from John F. Kennedy, a student of international conflict and unconventional warfare. Kennedy had read the works of Mao Tse Tung and Che Guevara, and he understood the changing nature of conflict away from nuclear confrontation to brush-fire wars. While the United States was reasonably well prepared for the former, he knew better than many of his generals and admirals how badly the US was prepared for unconventional warfare.

Kennedy was aware of the British success against guerrillas in Malaya in the late 1950s. The Brits learned to turn the guerrilla's tactics and strategies around on them, learned to live in the jungle—where they fought and won uncounted little battles. Kennedy perceived a warning and an opportunity. As a newly elected president, he was in a position to make things happen, and he did. He didn't invent the SEALs or the Green Berets—both organizations already existed but were allowed meager resources and roles.

The Army, in particular, loathed the fledgling special operations units that existed at the time. They refused to "play fair" in exercises and frequently disrupted the intended outcome. As a result, wearing the green beret was a court-martial offense at Fort Bragg—until Kennedy showed up. The Navy wasn't as parochial, but the UDTs were still hardly a barnacle on the chain of command.

Kennedy put the whole Department of Defense on notice that there was about to be a change of mission. The change was from a focus on a northern European, NATO versus Warsaw Pact conflict, to the kinds of wars Kennedy thought the US was likely to actually have to fight. He said, "This is another type of warfare, new in its intensity, ancient in its art—war by guerrillas, subversives, insurgents, assassins—war by ambush, instead of by combat—war by infiltration instead of aggression; seeking victory by eroding and exhausting the enemy instead of engaging him. And these are the kinds of challenges that will be before us in the next decade, if freedom is to be saved—a whole new kind of strategy, a wholly different kind of force, and therefore a new and wholly different kind of military training."

Kennedy insisted not only on new training, new organization, and new strategies, but on new weapons and equipment as well. He was responsible for the development and introduction of the AR-15/M16 rifle and the jungle boot, with its steel insert to protect against punji stakes. But it was the development of what became known as a *special warfare* capability within the US Department of Defense that was one of Kennedy's most inspired and enduring legacies.

The Army's Special Forces (known popularly but unofficially as the Green Berets) and the Navy's SEALs and SBSs share many things, including missions, heritage, and a strong sense of mutual respect. Both were developed, at Kennedy's insistence, in the early 1960s. At the outset, both were envisioned as extensions of the World War II Office of Strategic Services (OSS) teams that parachuted behind enemy lines to train, equip, lead, and inspire the native population, a catalyst that used a few men to put hundreds of soldiers in the field. It was called *unconventional*

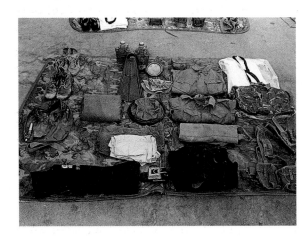

The basic issue of gear is laid out for inspection in this Vietnam-era photograph: coral shoes, canteens, flippers, weight belt, wet suit, web gear, uniforms, and unshined boots. Gary Stubblefield

warfare and it was a good idea. It worked—in some times and in some places.

Birth of the SEALs and SBSs

The SEALs were officially born on 1 January 1962, with President Kennedy doing the honors, commissioning Team One and Two, assigned to the Pacific and Atlantic theaters. The original mission was to conduct Naval Special Warfare—which then meant unconventional warfare, counterguerrilla and clandestine operations in maritime and riverine environments. This meant, theoretically, the capability to: 1) destroy enemy shipping and harbor facilities; 2) infiltrate and extract friendly force agents, guerrillas, and escapees; 3) conduct reconnaissance and surveillance; 4) conduct counterinsurgency civic action; 5) organize, train, and lead paramilitary forces.

The new organization got its first taste of real world operations shortly thereafter, conducting operations in support of the Cuban Missile Crisis in 1962, and again in 1965, in the Dominican Republic. Neither lasted long or received much attention, but both put the teams under the kind of pressure that only happens during genuine hostilities. It was a useful rehearsal for the big war that was about to begin. SEALs in small numbers shipped out to Vietnam in 1962, working out of Da Nang and functioning in an advisory role to the Vietnamese Navy, much as the Green Berets were doing for the Army of Vietnam at the same time.

SEAL Team One trained up and deployed two platoons to Vietnam in 1965, assigned to operate in the Rung Sat Special Zone near the capital city, Saigon. These platoons started operating in areas never previously visited by American or Vietnamese forces, deep in the mazes of rivers, creeks, and channels where the VC (Viet Cong, communist South Vietnamese rebels) had been safe. The platoons set up listening posts to collect information on VC activity and ambushes to turn the VC activity off.

The poor VC would come cruising back from a night on the town, shooting up the nearest government outpost, collecting "taxes" from farmers going to market, or assassinating mayors or other officials who might be friendly to Saigon, putting along a deserted stretch of canal in their sampans on the way back to base all fat, dumb, and happy. Then, suddenly, the canal bank would erupt as machine guns and rifles opened up from an artfully prepared ambush. The VC were either killed or captured, their operational routine disrupted, and their influence over the local population severely reduced. The American SEALs were turning a VC tactic around and using it effectively. It just wasn't fair, somehow! It was stealthy, sneaky, and utterly unexpected—just what Americans were not supposed to be able to do, setting the tone for the conduct of Naval Special Warfare to the present day.

The results from this preliminary experiment were quite successful, and four additional platoons were soon sent, two assigned to Nha Be, one to Binh Thuy, and another to My Tho. With a headquarters element, Detachment Alpha, set up at Subic Bay in the Philippines, the SEALs were ready to "lock and load." Detachment Bravo went aboard an APD as a component of a beach recon group, Detachment Charlie went aboard two fleet submarines (the USS *Perch* and USS *Tunney*), and Detachment Delta was sent to Da Nang, Republic of Vietnam. Detachments Echo and Foxtrot went aboard the Amphibious Ready Group standing off the coast, with assignments to assist with demolitions and beach surveys. But it was "Dets" Golf and Hotel, the riverine patrols, that most frequently closed with the enemy and where much of the legend of the SEALs in that war was built.

SEALs were again deployed to Vietnam in 1966, first to the area around Saigon and later to the rich, heavily populated Mekong Delta. The platoons did their workup together, deployed together, and returned together after six-month tours. This made for a kind of intimacy and unit cohesion far stronger than the main force Army units in the country at the time, where soldiers rotated in and out of units individually for one-year tours.

In some important ways, the lessons of the SEAL platoons and teams during the war in Vietnam have been ignored and overlooked. Within the limited areas in which they operated, these little units became highly effective in a generally ineffective war. Their efforts were independent of a larger strategy and so failed to have a lasting impact on the bigger campaign, but they did show what could—and still can—be done by extremely small, stealthy units operating in a maritime environment.

The platoons were given tremendous freedom to conduct their operations as they saw fit. They developed their own intelligence, plans, and procedures, and executed their missions pretty much without interference or support from the Army or Air Force or from the local Vietnamese military commanders.

Although they avoided working with the local Army of the Republic of Vietnam (ARVN) as much as possible, the SEAL teams often included Vietnamese SEALs. Some of these men were very good. They provided excellent translation services and often exhibited a high degree of combat discipline.

The most common and appropriate use of the SEAL teams were in ambushes, recon missions, and prisoner snatches. The small size of the units, even when supported with gunboats and ground-support aircraft, normally kept the platoons from engaging anything bigger than an enemy platoon or, if it couldn't be avoided, a company or even a battalion. Their

One of the most frustrating elements of combat operations in Vietnam was the way the VC and North Vietnamese Army (NVA) often used civilians for cover and concealment. Sorting out the good guys from the bad guys was always a problem, particularly within the heavily populated Mekong delta where SEALs did most of their operations. Gary Stubblefield

flexibility and experience, the effective and efficient support from the boat units, and the air and intelligence teams attached to the SEAL platoons all made for a successful fighting force and a style of operations that is extremely different than that used today.

In the Mekong Delta, particularly, SEAL operations ranged from simple ambushes to complex joint operations, staged from Navy ships located over the horizon, involving transit to the beach in small craft. SEALs used Army helicopter gunships, naval gunfire support, US Air Force "fast-movers," and Army helicopters again, this time the "slicks" for extraction from hot landing zones. SEALs also ran the Provincial Reconnaissance Units (PRUs) as part of the exotic Phoenix program.

Platoons at the time used fourteen men, but a typical mission usually called for no more than seven. Intelligence collection for an operation usually took several weeks and was developed concurrently with other operations. The platoon leader would design a mission around resources and objectives. Helicopters would be laid on for gunship fire support, the boats would be scheduled, an interpreter and a Vietnamese SEAL assigned. The helo crews were briefed, the squads received a warning order, and then, when the plan was fully refined, they got an operation order. Gary Stubblefield, a retired SEAL commander, says, "Briefings in those days took one hour, an hour and a half, max. We already knew our SOPs, we already knew our area. All we had to do was catch up with the changes required for the specific mission. The hard part was the 'actions at the objective' portion, where we got really detailed.

"Typically, we'd leave some time after dark, insert sometime before midnight, maintain an ambush until about daylight, break the ambush and get back in the boats to go back to the base."

A War Story

CAPT Bob Gormly has commanded SEAL Teams Two and Six, UDT-12, and NSW Group Two during a long career in Naval Special Warfare, just concluded. As a young lieutenant he went to Vietnam with SEAL Team Two's first deployment to the combat zone in 1967. SEAL Team Two was sent to the Mekong Delta, a hotbed of enemy activity, in the first use of the SEALs in that part of the country—though Team One had been working for some time up to the north, around Saigon.

"Our operations at first were kind of 'touch and feel,'" he says. "We were always searching for a strategy that we fitted into—and we never found it—but we had a lot of fun. Us young lieutenants had tremendous freedom about how we wanted to run an operation. We couldn't be told by anybody to run an operation that we didn't want to do."

Back then the entire delta was considered "Indian" country—hostile territory. The only real US presence was the Navy's River Patrol Force (CTF-116), which used PBRs to patrol the major rivers for about a year, getting shot at regularly. The VC had pretty much free run of the rest of the area.

The problem for the newly established SEALs from Team Two was first to find out what was going on. That required an intelligence information program, something that began immediately with requests for overflights, interrogations of prisoners, radio intercepts, and similar information-gathering techniques.

Gormly developed his own little plan for how he wanted to operate. First, the SEALs wouldn't go where other friendly forces could operate—because there probably wouldn't be anything there, and to make coordination with friendly forces more efficient.

After considering the available intelligence information—the "intel" as it's called—Gormly would call for a Navy Seawolf helicopter and go for a ride. He flew over the area he was interested in to get a sense of the lay of the land, looking for signs of enemy activity. Although there were no US forces in the area, other than CTF-116, there were a few trustworthy American officers in the delta who could help keep the chaos and confusion to a minimum.

"Then I'd land at the subsector headquarters to meet with the senior US advisor, usually a US Army captain or major, who would be working with the local Vietnamese provincial and subsector commanders. I'd walk in and tell him, 'Hi, I'm Bob Gormly. I've got a SEAL team, and we want to operate in your subsector—and I don't want anybody else to know about it but *you*.' To a man, they all agreed to that condition. Then I'd tell them, 'I'm going to be out there sometime in the next three or four days. I'm not going to tell you when. Just, please, don't put H & I [harassment and interdiction artillery fire] in there.'

"Then I'd go back to base, get the platoon together, start running whatever intel we had on the place, setting up to go. We usually went the next night.

"Just before we launched, within six hours, I sent a UNODIR [unless otherwise directed] message . . . a *flash* message that went to all higher headquarters that began 'Unless Otherwise Directed,' and indicated where we were going. Never once was I told not to go. Then we'd hop in the boat and head down river.

"We traveled very light, only small arms, plus an M60 machine gun and an M79 grenade launcher. The briefing was simple: I made sure everybody had the equipment they were assigned, then I told them where we were going, when, and what we were going to do. 'Any questions? No? Let's go!'

"We jumped in the boat, a twenty-two foot trimaran and took off. The boat was a 75mph boat that we made into a 25mph boat by adding a lot of weight in the form of ceramic armor, weapons, and a lot of people."

The SOP for ambushes involved cruising down one of the main rivers or canals into the general area of the objective, inserting several kilometers ("klicks," in the trade), and walking in to the ambush site along another canal. A typical mission involved a boat trip of fifty kilometers or so up the lazy river, as fast as possible for most of the trip, then as quietly and innocently as possible for the last few klicks. Navigation in the confused maze of canals was a tremendous problem, generally

one the skipper of the boat was responsible for. If he was good you arrived where you planned to go—if not, you could have a real problem.

The most dangerous and vulnerable concern was the problem of getting off the boat and into the local woodwork without being noticed. Nearly all insertions were done in the middle of the night. Rather than run the boat up into the weeds and debark the patrol in obvious fashion, the insertion was usually conducted in a more sneaky way. While the boat motored along in normal fashion, the team members merely stepped off the stern in patrol order, swam ashore, and slithered up on the bank. They all waited silently for ten minutes or so, listening for any movement that might indicate they'd been compromised and that enemy forces were moving in to investigate. If that happened, the boat could be recalled for an emergency extraction. Otherwise the mission proceeded according to SOP and to plan.

In the delta, the patrol would move out into the rice paddies, staying off the dikes and away from the treelines where enemy soldiers were most likely to be. Movement was extremely slow and careful, the SEALs moving quietly toward the intended ambush site, normally a canal bank, usually several klicks from the insertion point.

"Although we were in a free-fire zone where everything that moved at night was considered enemy," Gormly says, "we were more selective. Unless I actually saw weapons on the boats we would call the boat over to the bank and search it. If they were 'clean' I'd just take the sampan down the canal a ways and hold them there while we waited for somebody else to come along. One night we had to wait for four sampans before one came along that belonged to the bad guys."

SOP for that kind of contact was for the patrol leader to initiate the ambush, typically at quite short range where the M60, the M16s on full-auto, and the M79 grenade launcher's focused fire would shred the wooden vessel and its crew. The team would wait for the

From 1,000 feet overhead, the farms and rivers of the Mekong Delta look deceptively tranquil in this pre-op recon photo. Within the lush growth along the river are likely to be bunkers and fighting posi- *tions. Inland, among the fields and groves, may lurk more enemy facilities and stores—and the enemy himself.* Gary Stubblefield

leader to fire, sometimes with full-tracers, the signal to "hose down" the enemy vessel. "Seven guys carry a *lot* of firepower," Gormly recalls. "If it was a good hit and there were a lot of weapons aboard we might stick around to see what happened—maybe somebody would come over to investigate. Then we could ambush them too!"

After the patrol leader was satisfied with the evening's mayhem, the order to move would be given. The detained boats would be released, much to the relief of the fishermen aboard, and the SEALs would move off toward the extraction point. The pickup boat would already be somewhere in the vicinity for the scheduled recovery of the team, waiting for a radio call. The team would be recovered and would head back to base for debriefing and chow. In a couple of days it would be time for another briefing and another mission.

This pattern was used for the vast majority of SEAL missions of all types, including recons and prisoner snatches, with slight variations. Recons involved insertion around two or three in the morning, then patrolling into a predetermined overwatch location, setting up a "hide," and staying very still all day. Air or artillery fire could be called in on targets of opportunity. Finally, late at night, the SEALs would patrol back out to be extracted.

While this was a pretty efficient way of running operations, it was hardly without risk. Gormly was asked to send a team onto Cu Lao Tan Dinh, an island in the delta where enemy gunners routinely shot up passing patrol boats from fortified bunker complexes. With several patrol boats standing by for fire support, the team inserted at first light of 7 June 1967, loaded with hundreds of pounds of C4 explosive, blasting caps, detonation cord, and fuse.

Once ashore, Gormly's motley crew "sneaked and peeked" around for three or four hours, finding lots of bunkers in the process but not encountering any of the loyal opposing team. With the patrol boat supplying the demo materials, the team methodically blew up every bunker in sight. They did this for about four hours, moving steadily down the river from bunker site to bunker site. As they left what turned out to be the last bunker complex, Gormly noticed signs of human activity—bent grass where someone had stepped within the previous few minutes, leaving a trail away from the river. The patrol crawled thirty or forty meters forward, following the tracks, until Gormly (now on point) saw an enemy soldier, complete with helmet and weapon, in the weeds ahead. "I stood up and hosed him down. Then I got shot—and all hell broke loose! We had walked down the side of an L-shaped ambush—lucky us! We had a *big* firefight, then made our way back to the river where we directed fire on the VC until we could get a boat in to extract us. The helo gunships and the boats stayed there for about eight more hours, shooting it out with the VC. I got shot through the wrist. The guy that shot me was no more than five feet behind me. We had a Vietnamese SEAL with us, and he hosed that guy down. I was *real* lucky—he shot me over my right shoulder. At first I didn't even know I was shot. I thought my rifle had jammed and blown up—then I noticed the gaping hole in my wrist and realized I'd been shot. That was kind of a stupid op but it was fun for a while!" It also turned out to be worth a Silver Star for Gormly after his SEALs wrote him up for the award.

Grenada

After Vietnam the armed forces of the United States suffered another postwar decline and was—as so often in the past—unprepared for the kinds of real world operations that always seem to materialize. But the failed Iranian hostage mission, among other factors, had begun to revitalize the conventional armed forces when, on 23 October 1983, the SEALs went off to war again, kicking off Operation Urgent Fury in Grenada.

Urgent Fury was, sad to say, pretty much a "goatscrew" for US Special Operations Forces generally, and for the SEALs in particular. The SOF community and the National Command Authority learned many lessons from the operation, but (as usual) it took the bloodshed of the former to educate the latter.

Point Salines Recon Air Insertion

On "point" for Operation Urgent Fury was one platoon of SEALs from Team Six tasked with a recon mission of Point Salines, a thin point of land at the extreme southwest end of the island on which the Grenadans had constructed a new airfield. The platoon's mission objective was a preinvasion recon of sites for amphibious and airborne landings. Their plan, which they developed themselves, involved an insertion by parachute of the sixteen men and their PBL (Patrol Boat, Light—a mil-spec Boston Whaler speed boat) near a Navy destroyer, the *Clifton Sprague*. Once in the water, the SEALs were to find the boat, assemble aboard it, rendezvous with the *Sprague*, take on more SEALs and three US Air Force combat controllers, and slip ashore for the recon. Planning such a complicated operation is one thing; making it happen in the real world is another.

Everything went wrong: instead of jumping at last light, as planned, the mission was late by six hours and the SEALs jumped into pitch black night, making link-up with the boats and the men extremely difficult. Then, overloaded with equipment, the SEALs were driven deep below the surface of the water on landing. Despite the use of flotation devices, three SEALs drowned at the very beginning of the insertion phase of the op. Others survived by jettisoning as much gear as possible from their 100-pound-plus loads. On the surface, one of the two PBLs couldn't be found. The five survivors simply floated on the surface, unable to execute the mission, awaiting rescue that would come at dawn with the arrival of the *Sprague*.

One of the SEALs in the other squad drowned on landing. That squad managed to recover its PBL, collect its survivors, and begin the execution phase of the mission. They found the *Sprague*, linked up with the other personnel, and headed in to the beach—only to encounter an enemy patrol boat and withdraw back to the destroyer.

They tried again the next night. This time another patrol boat came by; the crew killed the engine of their PBL and waited silently for the threat to pass. When the patrol boat was safely out of range, the SEALs tried to start the engine again—without success. They floated, dead in the water, for eleven hours before the *Sprague* came along. The airfield recon mission was, as they say, a "learning experience."

But elsewhere another SEAL recon mission was going off with more success. Using a more conventional (and less risky) fast boat insertion technique, elements from SEAL Team Four operated in direct support of the Marine Amphibious Unit preparing to conduct an assault on the Pearls airport, in the midsection of the little island. Bus service for SEAL Team Four was provided by Seafox crews from Special Boat Squadron Twenty. Late on the evening of 24 October the Seafoxes, heavily armed with machine guns and grenade launchers, got the SEALs ashore.

One element moved off to scout the airfield while the other conducted a beach recon. The result was good news and bad news. The bad news was that the beach wouldn't work for an amphibious assault; the reef and surf made it too hazardous. There was more bad news, too: the airfield was well defended. But the good news was that the SEALs provided the information before the assault was launched, enabling the task force commander to execute Plan B, a heli-borne troop lift. (The Marines executed their part of the show with precision and grace—then got back on their ships and went off to their original mission in Lebanon).

Beausejour Radio Station Takedown

The SEALs had two other assignments: the first was a takedown of the radio station at Beausejour; the second was a rescue, with US Army Delta teams, of the imprisoned British Governor General, Sir Paul Scoon. Scoon was being held under house arrest by Cuban and Grenadan forces involved in the coup at Governor's House, on a hillside above St. Georges. Both went badly.

After difficulties with helicopter insertion at the radio station, the SEALs from Team Six successfully captured the facility and defended themselves, first from an enemy vehicle that blundered into their perimeter, and then from a counterattack force that included a potent, Russian-built BTR armored car. Although the BTR was killed, a lot of the infantry with it were not, and the SEALs had to beat a hasty withdrawal to the sea. After a successful escape and evasion, they made it to the water, swam out from the shore, and illuminated their infrared rescue strobes. The strobes, invisible to the naked eye but brilliant on thermal imaging systems used by the helos and ships, attracted attention quickly, and the team was quickly picked up. More lessons learned for all hands.

SEALs to the Rescue at Governor's House

Meanwhile, over at Governor's House, another learning experience was in progress.

A Patrol Boat, River (PBR) noses into the shoreline to de-bus a squad of SEALs. Swift, stealthy, surprising ops in the Mekong delta essentially turned guerrilla warfare around on the VC and NVA, keeping *them off balance and insecure. It was accomplished by a skillful combination of boat crews and SEAL teams, operating together in a way that still makes sense.* US Navy

First, the helicopter pilots couldn't even *find* the landing sites on the maps and photographs. Finally, after a lot of thrashing around, the sites were identified, but—oh joy—although they look usable in the aerial photographs, they turned out to be utterly unsuitable in reality. The defenders, alerted by all the activity overhead, had plenty of time to collect their weapons, ammunition, and a spot to work from. Then, instead of rolling over and playing dead as expected, they sat up and took

notice—and aim at the helicopters, which they then shot up.

A force of about two platoons of SEALs fast-roped to the ground and made a dash for the compound, quickly seized it from a light force of police, and collected the governor and his family and staff. They then took up defensive positions—just in time. Another reaction force, again using a BTR, arrived on scene, complete with about a platoon of infantry. With the BTR beating up Governor's House

45

After calling for help, the squad runs off the mountain—right through this tiny pass. Overhead are the NVA, momentarily distracted by Cobra gunships firing up their positions. The squad, expecting a shower of enemy grenades at any moment, is on the run. Lieutenant Gormly leads the way, followed by Clay Grady and Ed Bowen, none of whom are too thrilled about the op. Bob Gormly collection

with its heavy machine gun and the infantry maneuvering on the place, the rescue operation was not going *quite* according to plan.

Among the many missing items from the SEALs bag of tricks was the radio they intended to use to call up support from the many gunships in the air. Instead, all that was available was a low-power, short-range squad radio designed essentially for coordination within the platoon. But at least it could talk to the Rangers and other units in the area and, by a series of relays, the SEALs were able to

get an Air Force AC-130 Spectre gunship overhead.

When a Spectre fires, it is essentially turning a firehose on the target, but with bullets instead of water pouring from its 20mm Vulcan rotary cannon. It is equipped with systems that permit incredible accuracy and precision target identification. And when the Spectre opened up on the reaction force, the party was over for most of them. According to one report, the crew of the aircraft reported to the SEALs after a firing run, "I see twenty 'flappers' and 'kickers' and seven 'runners.'"

Although the assault on Governor's House was held at bay, the enemy force was not driven off. The SEALs and the governor were to wait all night to be rescued by the Marines, over twenty-four hours after the operation began. It was, in the vernacular, a learning experience again.

While these operations were hardly textbook examples of the art, they were typical of the "first blood" encounters of inexperienced units throughout history. They revealed many inadequacies in doctrine, training, equipment, planning, and execution. Those lessons were studied and learned by all the armed forces, and major changes were then applied. The essence of these was to improve the integration of all the US Special Operations Forces into one force with different, mutually supporting talents: the US Special Operations Command assembled from Army, Navy, and Air Force units in 1986.

Panama

By the time Operation Just Cause kicked off in Panama in December of 1989, USSOCOM had come a long way in the process of integrating US special operators. In addition to better planning integration, all the forces had experienced better funding and received more attention as the NCA shifted the nation's military focus away from the Warsaw Pact threat toward the little brushfire wars and terrorist threats that now seemed more dangerous.

SEALs had two major assignments during Operation Just Cause: the *Presidente Porras* mission described earlier, and a mission with a similar objective, disabling Noriega's Neville Jet at Punta Paitilla airport. While the first mission went off pretty much according to the plan, the airport mission was a disaster.

The jet was identified as one of several likely ways Noriega might escape the noose prepared for him. While there were many options possible for taking it out of his game plan, the mission was assigned to the SEALs. The SEAL team, basing its plan on guidance from a higher headquarters, decided to send two platoons onto the airfield to seize the aircraft. When H-hour was pushed up fifteen minutes for the whole operation, the SEALs found themselves trying to play "beat the clock" and losing. The force of approximately forty men was discovered on the airfield and engaged in the open by some PDF who knew their stuff. The Panamanians fired low, skipping their bullets across the concrete. The SEALs took many hits—four dead, eight wounded. Although the Neville Jet was essentially destroyed, by accident, in the engagement, the mission was hardly a success. It even took an hour and a half to get the wounded out. Another learning experience, and a bitter lesson for all concerned.

But they did learn from it, directly and from the "after-action reviews" that followed, formally and informally. As the commander of the operation said to one critic, "You weren't there!" And he has a point—it is easy to be an armchair admiral (or lieutenant commander) and a different matter to do it under fire.

Persian Gulf, Round One

Special operations forces generally get tapped to fight the little wars and smaller skirmishes that tend to be forgotten rather quickly by the public and historians. One of these little operations, designated Ernest Will/Prime Chance, involved SEALs in the Persian Gulf long before that big "drive-by-shooting" called Desert Storm. These operations deployed US forces, in and out of USSOCOM, to the Persian Gulf during the war between Iran and Iraq. The purpose of the oper-

ations was to keep the sea lanes clear and secure for the passage of oil tankers, a rather tall order since the belligerents were indiscriminate about just who they were attacking and their use of mines, missiles, and the occasional small attack boat.

CDR Gary Stubblefield was one of the SEALs sent to the Gulf. His responsibility was to establish a kind of floating base to support a wide variety of "trigger pullers" from the Army, Marine Corps, and Navy—along with Air Force controllers—in a demonstration of what has come to be known as "jointness." The Army personnel operated AH-6 "Little Bird" attack helicopters and 20mm Vulcan cannons, the Marines provided defense for the platform, and all of them cooperated as a kind of guard force for the strategic waterway. For Stubblefield, the mission was twofold: support the guard force in the area with a secure, well-provisioned platform, and use the barge as a platform to stage offensive operations against hostile forces when required.

It was an interesting little operation. Several oil platforms were used by the Iranians as bases for offensive operations against shipping; the Marines took out some of these.

The SEALs *tried* to take down a couple of oil platforms, and probably would have done it well and perhaps with minimal loss of life. Instead, though, the "prep" cannon fire on the platforms that was intended to soften them up resulted in both platforms blowing up while the SEALs were about to land. As Stubblefield says, "We were *supposed* to capture the people on the platforms. But the wrong ammunition was used by the [navy gunners]; they were supposed to use armor piercing but used incendiary instead. While we were in the helicopters, on the way into the platforms, we got word that they blew up. There was no way we could land on them."

Persian Gulf, Round Two

Operation Desert Storm/Shield was the acid test for all the changes that had been incorporated in the US armed forces during the 1980s. SEALs and SBS crews played an active, early, and extremely successful role in

Urban combat skills have been a part of the SEALs' bag of tricks since the rise of terrorist groups and the necessity of hostage rescue operations began in the 1970s. This SEAL from Group Two is rehearsing his moves during a training op during Desert Storm. US Navy

the campaign.

One SEAL platoon, commanded by LT Tom Dietz, set up shop at a small naval base near the northern Saudi town of Ras al Mishab. After the air war kicked off in mid-January of 1991, the platoon started an aggressive reconnaissance program along the Kuwait coastline. Four special reconnaissance missions were executed, looking for any and all information about enemy defenses: Were there patrol boats operating in the area? Navigation aids still in place? Then, moving in closer to the beach, what kind of defenses were visible from offshore?

These recon missions had two or three phases. The first was supported by the SBS crews using their extremely fast, low, "cigarette" racing boats—designated HSBs (high-speed boats)—for a fast tour of the area. Although not really designed for the recon mission, the HSBs are normally tasked with training the bigger ships in the fleet against anti-ship attacks from such small, fast vessels, and they don't have an official tactical mission. But that speed made them excellent for these recons. With a Zodiac CRRC lashed to the deck, the boats made nighttime forays along the coastline. Dietz says, "We didn't know if there was going to be an amphibious invasion or not. We were told to look for a beach where one could be conducted—or where a deception operation could be conducted."

The first two missions identified two possible invasion beaches from well offshore. The next two missions sent the SEALs ashore to scout the defenses. The plan for the recon missions used two Zodiac inflatables for the run into the beach each night. There were sixteen guys in each platoon, who all wanted to go in, but only room for five in each Zodiac; Dietz had to decide who would go in the Zodiacs and who would stay in the HSBs. "It wasn't an easy decision," he says. "I integrated everybody into the missions, and everybody got to go, but there were some guys that went in every night and some that got rotated."

Three SEALs surface swam in to each beach, without scuba or closed circuit breathing apparatus, which seemed unnecessary. Despite the wet suits they all wore and the training and experience they'd developed, all were chilled. As Dietz says, "The difficult thing about these missions was the cold. We were wet the whole time, from dusk until around dawn. That's why we go through BUD/S and why we go through Hell Week—so we can be wet and tired and still think!"

The Zodiacs were put in the water from about ten miles out, then sent in to about a thousand meters offshore where the swimmers slid over the side into the chilly, low 50-degree water. The SEALs surface swam into the beaches, but not out of the surf. They lay on the sand, using the water for cover and concealment, watching and waiting for about an hour. Then, on schedule, they slipped back into deeper water and back out to the Zodiacs.

After reviewing the results of the intelligence collection missions, one particularly suitable beach was selected, just north of a point called Mina Sa'Ud. The fourth mission went in to the selected beach to confirm the assumptions of the earlier recons. Dietz, as platoon commander, went ashore to have "eyes on" the target, still not knowing if the platoon was supporting an actual invasion or a deception operation. Finally, the decision was made: execute the deception plan.

The plan for the deception operation called for three Zodiacs, and all the men in the platoon would be committed to the mission. Six would swim ashore, a swim pair from each boat; another three would stay behind to provide support. They were to install charges along the selected beach, primed with individual timers set for a two-hour delay. These charges were all supposed to detonate at about 0100 on the day the ground phase of Desert Storm kicked off, with coalition forces crossing their lines of departure at 0400. At about the same time the SBS crews and SEALs would close on the same beaches and fire them up with every suitable weapon they owned.

The charges and the gunfire didn't need to kill anybody or destroy anything to be effective. All they had to do was get the attention of the Iraqis and convince them that the Marines, who had been waiting offshore for just such an opportunity, were about to come across the beaches in a classic amphibious assault. If such an invasion actually happened and there was no one to meet it, the enemy commanders knew, the war would be over almost instantly.

But if there were no invasion and the enemy forces were still defending against one, that meant there were fewer enemy assets available to deal with the real assault, coming across the border to the west. So the SEAL platoon's sixteen men, plus the SBS crews in the HSBs, had the opportunity to take two whole divisions out of the war (about 20,000 enemy soldiers) with what amounted to a military version of a practical joke.

Execute The Deception Mission

"I've been asked how I picked the 'lucky' six who went in," Dietz says. "I basically chose the nine people who needed to stay back in the boats—my three best engine guys, three best machine gunners, three best radio operators—and the other six were left. But on the final operation I was able to take everybody. That's because we *needed* everybody."

Although the SEALs didn't see the need for Draeger scuba gear, they each took along a little "bail-out bottle" of air sufficient for about three minutes sub-surface swimming in case they made serious contact with any enemy defenders. The bottles were the kind of "field ex-

Desert Storm was a new test of Naval Special War-
fare people, tactics, and equipment. This RIB is
being prepared for a night operation in the Persian
Gulf.

pedient" solution to a problem that seems to materialize during war—they'd been acquired from a helicopter unit and adapted to an entirely different use (and a prohibited one) than that for which they were designed.

Of the six SEALs who swam in, three carried CAR-15s, the compact version of the M16A2 with a shorter barrel and a stock assembly that could be retracted. The CARs all had M203 grenade launchers attached for serious, long-range, indirect fire. The other three carried the German Heckler & Koch MP5 submachine gun with suppressers (not silencers) attached. "The idea was that if a couple of sentries showed up on the beach, and we thought we were compromised, we could take them out with the suppressed weapons without giving away our positions," Dietz says. "But if something heavy opened up on us—a machine gun, for example—at longer range, we could lay some grenades on it."

Each of the six swimmers carried a Mk 138 satchel charge. Two timers were attached to each, set for two hours. This kind of "double priming" is SOP. In the bags were ten two-pound blocks of C4 explosive, dual primed, the charges all carefully prepared ashore before everybody climbed into the water.

The swimmers went in to the beach on line, about twenty feet apart. Once they could touch bottom with their flippers, they spread out, about fifty meters from each other across the 250-meter-wide beach. "You could just see the guy on either side of you," Dietz says, "and we didn't have to wait for any signals. Once we spread out, we swam into the beach and placed our charges in about one foot of water—since the tide was now receding—pulled the pins on the timers and swam back out to regroup." The Zodiacs, which had been standing by about 500 meters off the beach, were signaled in for the pickup. Once the swimmers were hauled aboard, the "rubber ducks" headed out into the Gulf, about seven miles off the beach, to the rendezvous point with the supporting SBS crews in the speedy HSB cigarette boats.

Four of the HSBs participated in the operation. Two HSBs collected the Zodiacs and the SEALs, counted noses, and secured the inflatables. In the meantime, the other two zipped in to about two miles. Now, at about 0030 hours, the active part of the deception plan began as the two HSBs closed to 500 meters of the shoreline and opened up with every weapon aboard: mini-guns, heavy machine guns, grenade launchers. "They ripped the beach apart," according to the platoon leader. The firing continued for about ten noisy minutes. For any Iraqis ashore, this would obviously not be bombing or naval gunfire, but a large scale, close in attack of the type preceding an amphibious assault. On their final pass up the beach, the HSBs chucked several additional explosive charges overboard—more C4, wrapped in plastic, primed to go off in the water at irregular intervals. These detonated as the boats made a break for the exit. About five minutes later, almost exactly at the scheduled hour of 0100, the satchel charges ashore started exploding. All went off within about thirty seconds of each other, with a series of tremendous *booms* that were audible far out to sea, where the HSBs beat a hasty strategic withdrawal.

All four linked up out at the seven-mile mark, then headed back to base. At 0230 they debriefed. "It was a very low-key, matter-of-fact debrief," Dietz says. "The operation went according to plan. We were happy but not really excited about it. What we were really excited about was that the ground war was now kicking off! It wasn't until later, after we'd gotten cleaned up and had something to eat, that we got a message from CAPT (now RADM) Smith, the Task Group commander, reporting that elements of two Iraqi divisions remained on the coastline even as the ground forces were going up behind them. They remained in position to defend against the amphibious invasion. That's what really pleased us—that the Iraqis paid attention to us, reacted to us, and hopefully we saved some lives."

Chapter 3

Earning Your Flippers at BUD/S

So you think you wanna be a SEAL? No problem—piece of cake. Anybody can do it! It only takes twenty-six weeks, and the training is mostly done on the beautiful, sandy beach at Coronado, California, right on the Pacific Ocean near warm, wonderful San Diego, and the program is run by a large, kindly, attentive, cheerful, and well-trained staff of SEALs. There are always plenty of beautiful women strolling by to admire the handsome sailors; the famous and luxurious Hotel Del Coronado, with its superb restaurants and bars, is right down the road. There is plenty of sailing, surfing, scuba diving, and other recreation available in the immediate vicinity. The beach is always available for a nice jog. And, best of all, every instructor at the Basic Underwater Demolition/SEAL program is committed to making sure that every day of those twenty-six weeks are just *loaded* with activities and experiences you will *never* forget. Sound like fun? Sign right here!

Well, Navy recruiters don't actually sell

One of the first and most terrifying tests of BUD/S is called "drown-proofing." This involves spending a half an hour or so in the water—with your hands tied behind your back, floating at the surface, coming up for a breath, and then relaxing for a bit underwater. These students are practicing the maneuver before the test. They'll also have to retrieve the masks without using their hands, which are tied behind them.

prospective recruits that rosy view of the program. But despite many cautions, SEAL candidates often show up at BUD/S without a realistic understanding of what is actually involved in the training required to earn the "Budweiser" trident emblem of a SEAL. The truth is that it is one of the most difficult, challenging, and actually brutal learning experiences anybody can have, and one of the things most people learn is that they don't really want to be a SEAL quite badly enough to finish the program.

Like the Army's Green Beret Qualification Course (or Q Course), BUD/S is a *selection* and training program that weeds out people who don't belong. That usually means most of them. They are weeded out the only way that anybody has ever found for reliably selecting people who can hack the problem—by cranking up the stress so high that only the strongest survive and the quitters quit—or break. It is not nice and it isn't pretty. There isn't any other way. And sometimes it results in nearly everyone of an entering class of SEAL candidates being eliminated. In one class *not one* single man graduated. It is a calculatedly brutal experience that is not pretty to watch and pushes its victims to their limits of physical and emotional endurance, and beyond. Injuries are routine and deaths in training occasionally occur.

But, in a way, it is true that anybody can

When BUD/S students take a swim test it is not always a heap of fun. This class is about to be tested on drown-proofing skills.

survive it—if they have the appropriate state of mind. It takes plenty of strength, but most of it isn't muscular; it's mental. Little scrawny guys that you'd never pick for a badminton team sometimes turn out to have more of the kind of internal toughness and physical strength that it takes to survive BUD/S and become a SEAL than the big weight lifters who seem to be naturals. If you've got the mental strength to work through the discomfort, the fatigue, and the humiliation, you can probably develop the physical strength, SEALs tell you. The head is the hard part. And no other test has, so far, been able to figure out how to find the men who won't quit from those who will without pushing them

both far beyond the normal limits of civilized routine.

The BUD/S training takes twenty-six weeks, but it is only one part of the process of becoming a fully qualified SEAL. Before even applying for training a prospective candidate must: pass the very strict physical examination for Navy divers; have eyesight at least 20/40 in one eye and 20/70 in the other, correctable to 20/20, without color blindness; score high on military written tests; be male, twenty-eight years of age or less; and pass the physical fitness test (extremely high scores are expected) that includes swim test (500 yards, breast or side stroke, in less than 12:30), rest for ten minutes, then at least forty-two

Out on the "grinder," BUD/S students get an hour or two of formal physical training (PT) everyday. They get another ten hours or so of informal PT, too, paddling the rubber ducks, running up and down the beach, and frolicking around the obstacle course. During all this they are all expected to show a high degree of enthusiasm, no matter how miserable they may feel.

One of the kind and attentive staff of highly trained instructors helps a boat crew with their motivation. The technique is simple—a paddleful of sand, applied directly to the problem. Sand, it turns out, is a readily available, cheap, apparently effective material for helping people with their problems. It can be shoveled into boats and on hats, and the students can be rolled around in it, like a sugar cookie.

pushups in two minutes, at least fifty situps in two minutes, eight pullups, and run a mile and a half in boots and BDU pants in 11:30—all in less than an hour.

Applicants must come from certain Navy ratings, have the endorsement of their commanders, and have plenty of time remaining on their enlistment. If you fit all these require-

ments you can apply, and you might even be accepted and assigned a slot in a class. If that happens, don't wait to start your physical conditioning program. You don't go to BUD/S to get in shape; you *arrive* in shape, or you will fail almost instantly. "In order to even apply," RADM Ray Smith says, "you've got to be a top-notch sailor. We've got the pick of the guys coming out of the Naval Academy, more enlisted applicants than we can handle."

Although the published standards call for a cutoff age of twenty-eight, older men are sometimes accepted, and some are even recruited. Two thirty-six year olds have completed the program, and at least one man was thirty-two at the time. While the older bodies are a little less resilient sometimes, that can sometimes be offset by greater maturity and better self-discipline. One of these, a Polish refugee with extensive language skills, a former teacher and, at the time a competitive gymnast, was recruited for the program and made it through training on the first try.

New arrivals will indeed see the marvelous Hotel Del Coronado, the pretty sailboats, the girls sunbathing on the beach, and the glittering Pacific Ocean and will soon learn to loathe them all. They will soon learn that the Pacific is freezing, that the beach is for running on and rolling in, that the girls and the tourist attractions exist only as torture devices.

For seven long weeks the trainees endure a program of indoctrination and physical preconditioning, with long hours of classes, running, swimming, situps, pushups, calisthenics. They sweat and struggle . . . but they still haven't started BUD/S yet.

The Only Easy Day Was Yesterday

Phase One of BUD/S is the basic physical and mental conditioning portion of the program. It lasts nine weeks. It features a lot of running, swimming, and trips around the obstacle course. Every trainee is required to put his maximum effort into every test, every time. The minimum scores are raised each week. Each trainee is required to improve on his previous scores. Instructors watch and evaluate every hopeful trainee like hawks—or vultures—ready to pounce on any flaw or failure, real or imagined. It is an extremely abrasive, competitive process. The only way the instructors will leave you alone is if you've just beaten everybody else at an event; then you might be allowed a few minutes to gloat and relax while the rest of the class thrashes around in the surf zone.

This continues for five weeks. Each day the heat is turned up a little more. The instructors push harder and harder. The instructors never let up for a moment. As they say over and over, "The only easy day was *yesterday!*"

The students spend lots of time in the water, and the water is cold, even in summer. Hypothermia is a fact of life and occasional death. Wet suits are sometimes used, sometimes not; even with the suits, the cold Pacific Ocean seeps in, lowering body temperature. Students can be seen shivering violently sometimes after having come out of the cold ocean to stand in the cold wind. It is another stress, intentionally applied.

One by one people quit or are removed for injuries. Even quitting isn't easy, quick, or dignified; the trainee stands on the green painted frog footprints at one side of the "Grinder," the big blacktop space where calisthenics are performed, grasps the lanyard for the brass ship's bell attached to a column, rings the bell three times, and is gone. His green helmet liner remains in formation beside the bell with the others who've quit before him. While there is some disgrace to it, even these men get some credit (in private, away from the trainees) that it takes quite a man to get through any of BUD/S and that only a very select group even manage to get in the front door. While the quitters get credit for trying they are, just the same, an example to those who remain.

The O Course

One of the featured entertainments is the obstacle course—the "O course" in SEAL par-

"Get it up! Get that boat up! Get it up! Get it up! You guys are the worst—get it up!" the instructor screams. After their first jaunt out into the Pacific in the rubber ducks, a crew has a few moments of quiet reflection on what they've seen and done—their newfound skills in small-boat handling and teamwork, with the help of the staff providing a running commentary and critique. After a few minutes supporting the 250-pound boat aloft, the crew tends to have an improved understanding of the lessons of BUD/S.

lance. It looks like a big sandbox with lots of play equipment: telephone poles assembled into a wide variety of structures. The BUD/S trainees are assembled here about once a week for an hour or two of play time. One after another, on command, the students dash off for a circuit of the course.

You start by running to the first event, a set of pole stumps set in the ground, their tops about two feet above the deck. You must run across them, jumping from one to the next without falling off. Then, from the last stump, leap to the top of a low wall, swing a foot over, drop to the other side, and start running. You'll go about fifty feet before you dive under a grid of barbed wire—crawl under the wire, then emerge and dash to the next structure, the net climb. A tall tower suspends a rope net that you climb to the top, swing over, and descend; the flexible net offers unstable footing and it is slow going. Once safely back on the ground, dash off to the next position, a pair of simple structures about four feet apart; you climb up on one and jump to the other, catching the crossbar across your chest; this is a favorite way to break a rib. They call this one "The Ugly Name." There are about ten more obstacles to negotiate, and your progress will be closely monitored by one of the attentive, helpful staff who are always ready with words of encouragement and advice. If you have trouble with part of the course the instructors will probably let you try the event all over again, just to make sure you get it right. Finally you return to your starting point and your time is recorded.

If you haven't done well you may get to cool off with a quick dip in the ocean, on the other side of a tall sand berm. Then, to dry off, you'll be expected to roll in the sand, then hustle back to rejoin the play group. As the trainees quickly learn, the O course is highly competitive, and people who don't do well are subject to extra, undesired, attention from the instructors.

You're expected to go all out every time you run the course, and you're expected to do better every week. Minimum times for the course are published, and they get shorter every week. It is just one of the stresses that

Look like fun? The obstacle course tests strength, agility, and speed—and mental toughness, too. All are expected to improve over the weeks, and a trainee's times must get progressively better.

are applied to the trainees to test their motivation and physical conditioning. But, as one of the staff says, "It isn't supposed to break you but to build up your confidence. It reveals a lot about the character of an individual. By the time you've gone through about three-fourths of it, every fiber of your muscles is burning, and you still have another quarter to go—and it's all through soft sand."

Hell Week

After five weeks of this comes the real

The circuit begins with a dash across the tops of these poles, a leap to the wall, over the wall to crawl under some barbed wire, then off to the net climb. It takes about eleven minutes to do them all, if you're in shape. The instructors provide helpful comments and critiques at most stations.

challenge that all have heard about and dreaded: Hell Week. It starts just before midnight on the Saturday before the sixth week with a gentle wakeup call from the instructors . . . using blank M60 machine gun fire and artillery simulators as an improvised alarm clock. The noise in the compound is deafening. Besides the firing, instructors scream incessantly. Chaos reigns supreme.

The trainees begin five and a half days of virtually constant activity. They will receive an average of about twenty minutes sleep per day, if they are lucky. They will go from one event to another, constantly: running on the beach, boat drills, PT, swims. They will crawl in slime, roll in the surf, and for a little extra torture, do "log PT."

Log PT requires boat teams to lift and maneuver sections of log weighing from 400 to 600 pounds. If your boat team hasn't been doing well (or if the instructors think you need a little extra help with your motivation), you'll get the 600-pound model. Then you can do situps with it on your chest, or try holding it over your head for a while. Needless to say the whole team has to work together to do anything with it at all.

The sun comes up on the first morning, and the day proceeds much like any other at BUD/S. The sun goes down, and the trainees know that somewhere people are returning to homes and wives, to quiet evenings and friendly conversations. In the tall apartment buildings overlooking the BUD/S compound the lights will start going out around nine or ten. The PT continues. By 1:00 a.m. they are nearly all out, but the activity on the beach continues. "The only easy day was *yesterday!*" scream the instructors.

When the sun comes up the next morning, the trainees will be a bit tired but will try not to think about it. All of them know what the routine is, that the really tough part is still days away. The competitions continue with boat races in the ocean and on the bay. Gradually, individuals will fail. When they do, their teams are subjected to more stress from the instructors and from the other teams.

A recipient of the "sugar cookie" treatment—first get wet in the surf, then roll around in the sand. Then get back in line and try to do better. It's just one of the constant stresses and strains on trainees designed to separate those who will tolerate it from those who won't.

Although they don't get any real sleep, the trainees get plenty of food. They consume about 7,000 calories a day and still lose weight.

One day melts seamlessly into another without rest. There is no alternative but to tough it out, drive through the fatigue, and keep doing what they tell you to do. It is a test of mental toughness as much as the powers of physical endurance. After four days or so people start to hallucinate. And some people start

Log PT is another form of stress, this time applied to a whole boat crew all at the same time. US Navy

to quit. Hell Week is the most important part of the whole twenty-six week BUD/S experience, a physical and mental challenge that is intended to put the trainees under stress that is supposed to approach that of actual combat.

The hallucinations can be rather entertaining. While enduring a long night boat race out on the ocean, after a few days with no sleep and little rest, visions begin to appear. Sometimes it is mermaids, other times people picnicking on the beach, or a strange tunnel vision.

One of the rituals is the letter home. Toward the end of the week, when everybody is off in the ozone, they are all seated before tables and provided paper and pen. "Write me a letter explaining why you want to become a SEAL!" the instructor orders. This is not an easy thing to explain after going three or four days without sleep, wallowing in the mud, doing log PT, enduring endless boat drills, and slogging through competitive events like the "rubber duck" races on the ocean or the sixteen-mile runs on the beach. The students tend to stare at the paper for a while before attempting to write anything. The results tend to be gibberish. Later, after Hell Week is over, these essays are returned to their authors as an amusing reminder of the tremendous stress they were under and how it affected their performance of even this simple task.

As rough as Hell Week and the whole BUD/S program is, it has been toned down considerably from the past. Trainees no longer

Hell Week features rest breaks in the mud pit. Well, not really rest breaks but opportunities to work on your teamwork . . . and practice being miserable.

Not only do these guys get to stay awake for five and a half days straight, they get to do fun stuff like this day and night.

This is their first experience with a rubber duck in the ocean, dealing with the surf and having to function as a crew. Most will do rather badly and will overturn in the surf, lose paddles, and sometimes lose a man over the side. The instructors enjoy it all immensely—and pile on the punishment.

have to wallow in the mud of the Tijuana River, essentially an open sewer, after many came down with severe (and sometimes permanent) illnesses. That ended in 1983. A somewhat healthier goo is now available right in San Diego Bay. And after one trainee died on a five-mile winter swim around San Clemente Island, the staff started taking extra precautions to deal with extreme overexertion and hypothermia. An ambulance now trails along the beach behind the trainees on the long runs through the soft sand, trailing the "goon squad," as the slower runners are called; they can quit at any time, and many do.

BUD/S has been criticized, along with other extreme selection and training programs like the Army's Green Beret Q Course, for unnecessary extremes. The injuries, the high level of stress, the humiliation are all far more than anyone in civilian life or in normal military training ever must endure.

Why do it that way? As one SEAL officer explains, "One of the things I've noticed about many of the 'real world' combat operations I've been on is that you get a tremendous adrenaline rush—I call it *fear*. Once the operation begins that goes away, but on the way in you have a lot of time to sit and think. You *never* get that in a training situation! So one of the things I continually tell my troops while we are training is, 'Look, I can't give you the feeling of what it is really like to be in combat . . .

The famous bell is always waiting for anybody who's had enough. Then, you stand on the green frog footprints, grasp the lanyard, and strike the *bell three times—and you can go back to the regular Navy, to conventional hours and conventional missions.*

because I can't shoot at you and make you hurt. It's illegal, and I wouldn't want to do that anyway. What I *can* do is to make the conditions so tough, and try to make you so tired, put you under such stress, that you will get something of a feeling of what it is like."

When the trainees recover from Hell Week they begin a period of study intended to prepare them for "hydrographic reconnaissance," as beach surveys are called. This involves even more time spent wallowing around in the surf, cold and miserable, while the ever-attentive staff offers suggestions and encouragement from the beach. Once through Hell Week students are treated with a bit more respect and affection by the instructors. Finally, Phase One is over.

Swim fins, mask, and booties are all pretty much standard commercial gear, used in unconventional diving.

Phase Two

Survivors of the first part of training go on to Phase Two, where they will learn about diving operations. Each will learn just about all there is to know about scuba, closed-circuit rebreathing systems, and dive physiology. They will learn more than they ever wanted to know about the nasty things that happen to people who make mistakes underwater. They learn to deal with equipment failures, lost regulators, the hazards of nitrogen narcosis. They make long swims beneath the surface and learn to navigate in the cold, murky, dark waters in which SEALs operate. After seven busy weeks the BUD/S class will be missing a few more faces. The survivors will have the knowledge necessary to be basic combat divers, and the program is about to get really interesting.

Phase Three

By now the BUD/S class is beginning to see light at the end of the proverbial tunnel, and are pretty sure it is not from an oncoming train. They are far stronger physically and mentally than four months earlier. They've acquired a great deal of knowledge and confidence. Now they get to start putting the skills and the stamina together in practical exercises that simulate SEAL missions.

Phase Three is the Demolitions/Recon/Land Warfare part of the program. The BUD/S students learn land navigation, explosives, small unit tactics, rappelling, and patrolling skills and become expert in the employment of all the small arms and weapons used by SEALs in combat. After four weeks of classroom instruction and practical exercises, the trainees deploy to San Clemente Island for five weeks, where they put it all together.

One of the evolutions involves clearing beach obstacles like those that faced the amphibious operations of World War II—concrete blocks and steel rails dropped in shallow water to block the passage of landing craft. The students first make a careful hydrographic survey of the landing zone, noting the location of all obstacles, then plan a mission to demolish them with explosives. The quantity of

A "stick" of jumpers exits a Navy CH-46 helicopter. All SEALs are jump-qualified after they complete

BUD/S at the US Army's Basic Airborne Course at Fort Benning, Georgia.

explosive has to be carefully calculated, fuse measured. The students use their "rubber ducks" to get into the area, then dive to emplace the explosives. All the charges are linked with "det" cord to insure simultaneous explosion, and the divers are recovered to the boats. The last dive pair pulls the safety pins on the fuse-lighters, retracts the striker, and pops the igniter. Now it is time to get back to the boat. The instructors will time the delay, and it had better be within a few seconds of what was calculated. With a satisfying *whump* the surface of the water will boil, and the obstacles will (usually) be shattered.

BUD/S is probably the roughest, most demanding training and selection program in the US armed forces, at least outside the covert organizations. It has been loudly criticized as excessively brutal. Although it might not be quite as dangerous as at times in the past, it is a guaranteed way to get miserable fast and stay miserable for most of six months—or more, if you get injured. And the injuries are common, almost with the intent of the staff. No other program tolerates such a high level of injuries. A lot of people outside Naval Special Warfare think the BUD/S program is sadistic and ought to be reformed. CDR Gary Stubblefield has an opposing view:

"It is the toughest military training in the world, and it's done that way on purpose. The Army's Special Forces don't have anything to compare to it. It's been this way since the days of the Scout and Raiders in World War II, a *very* difficult selection process. Most of the people who make it through the program are not premier athletes—they are *normal* people who have the ability to stick with something.

"There are injuries, some severe, in every class. But the business we are in is inherently dangerous, combat or not. If you take away the risk that goes with the training, you take away the mental stress that you put people under to know how they'll respond in the real world, in actual combat. Landing on rocks, long cold swims, surf passages—training where we have people break arms and legs—has to be part of the program. You *have* to be sure that they will stick with you when the going gets tough, and they have to know that, if you don't do things safely, there are consequences that include injury . . . or worse. Death in training is very, very rare, and it happens, I think, when the student doesn't follow the rules. The deaths are an anomaly but the injuries are not—those happen when someone does something they aren't supposed to."

Jump School

But even after surviving BUD/S, a trainee is still not a fully qualified SEAL and does not wear the trident insignia of Naval Special Warfare. First comes three weeks at the US Army's Fort Benning in Georgia, undergoing the Basic Airborne Course. Here each will have to confront a different fear, that of jumping from an airplane, to become a fully qualified military parachutist.

The first week involves physical conditioning, and since the Army school's standards are comparatively low, the BUD/S graduates manage this part of the program more or less with one hand tied behind their backs. The Army instructors will try to make the experience a little bit challenging for any SEALs, Rangers, Marines, or others they can identify, usually requiring extra PT to keep their attention, but BUD/S graduates generally consider this part of the program a kind of vacation.

Week two teaches the basic skills of military parachuting: donning the parachute, actions inside the aircraft, door position, jumpmaster commands, proper exit techniques, emergency procedures, and the Parachute Landing Fall (PLF). The students endlessly practice door position, exits, and PLFs from training aids: the suspended harness, the thirty-four-foot tower, the C-130 mock-up.

Finally, they start week three, Jump Week. Five jumps are required, three "Hollywood" daylight jumps without combat equipment plus one night jump and one jump with loaded rucksack and weapons container. The night jump is usually a sunrise or sunset jump rather than one in full darkness.

Jump school is actually a lot of fun for many of the people who attend, and the BUD/S graduates hardly work up a sweat. The jumps are often exciting, the instructors fairly civilized, the drop zone a soft, fluffy plowed field. The last jump is generally done on Friday morning, and students often invite friends and relatives to watch from nearby bleachers. Then the Army instructors break out the silver wings of a qualified military parachutist and pin them to the shirts of the students.

The "Budweiser"

Completion of the Basic Airborne Course is the final academic portion of the program required to join a SEAL or Swimmer Delivery Vehicle (SDV) team but the students are still not bona fide SEALs. First, each man is assigned to a team where he must complete a six-month probationary period. It is still possible to fail, and individuals occasionally are filtered out, even now, if they don't fit into the

The Naval Special Warfare trident insignia (the "Budweiser" in the SEAL vernacular) is awarded only after completion of BUD/S, airborne training, and a probationary period on a SEAL team that lasts from six months to more than a year.

team or fail to meet spec somehow. But at the end of the six months, a year or more after starting the process, a few young men will pin on the big, gold symbol of Naval Special Warfare and finally be able to call themselves SEALs.

They enter a tiny, select community with a big reputation that sometimes gets in the way of business. Within the military SEALs are sometimes known as "cowboys" or "glass-eaters" who glory in their superman image. Instead they find a different kind of man on the teams: extremely confident without bravado, a man with tremendous talents and abilities, a person who knows his own limits. "We like to think of ourselves as quiet professionals," one says.

RADM Ray Smith says: "We are essentially a *people* business. We use a lot of exotic equipment—scuba, parachutes, radios—but all those things are peripheral to the essence of what we are. Our focus at BUD/S is on the human being, the nature of the person we want to have come on a SEAL team and do the things we have to do—always has been, always will. The finest equipment in the world (which we have) is not sufficient to accomplish our missions. You'll see guys in BUD/S who don't look very impressive physically—little guys, young guys—who'll surprise you and make it through. You can *never* successfully predict who will make it through! You can't measure what is inside the individual without subjecting him to BUD/S. In fact, this is a course in the development of human potential; all we are trying to do is to make the young man understand that the limits of the human being are practically unlimited."

Of the fifty or sixty students who begin BUD/S, the staff will tell you there will be five or six who *know* that they are going to complete the program, no matter what, and that there is no stopping them. There is another five or six who don't really want to be here, are not really ready for the challenge, and who will never be SEALs. In the middle are the eighty percent the instructors focus their efforts on. They probe for the fears that every

BUD/S is a selection process more than a training program, challenging people to use far more of their personal resources than most will ever need to do. It is a rather brutal program, by design, intended to help people survive and function in the far more brutal and stressful environment of combat.

man has—a fear of heights, of water, of jumping from high platforms—and each is confronted daily with his perceived limitations and pushed past them. "You can't call 'time out' in combat," one of the instructors says, "and that's what we try to teach them here."

Officers and enlisted personnel go through training together, unlike some other programs where officers sometimes get an easier ride. Both suffer and perform equally at BUD/S. It is a team-building system, developing trust up and down the chain of command. About thirty-five new officers and 250 enlisted personnel graduate from BUD/S annually and join the world of SPECWARCOM on the SEAL, Special Boat, and Swimmer Delivery Vehicle teams.

Chapter 4

Movement to Contact

Despite the way it is shown in the movies, the business of going into combat is a lot more complicated than picking up your weapon and following some resolute-looking lieutenant or sergeant who growls, "Okay, men, follow me!" The movies always manage to leave out all the paperwork, meetings, and related homework that comes first. In fact, it is just about impossible for American combat units to go off to battle without a great deal of this stuff. It can take weeks to prepare an operation of any kind, conventional or covert, but at the end of this long process will finally come two quite interesting "management/staff" meetings. The first of these is called a Warning Order; the other is called the Patrol Leader's Order.

The Warning Order

Before SEALs and SBS crews go anywhere or do anything, the mission has to be authorized, approved, and planned. A long time ago the units did most of this internally, but for the last decade or so, the missions have been conceived and tasked from outside NAVSPECWARCOM. Somewhere during the process somebody decides it is okay to actually

A swim pair secure the beach. Depending on the mission, SEALs wear wet suits or standard uniforms (which will be wet suits, too, in a way). The man on the left is one of the more unusual members of the special ops community—a "long hair" SEAL.

let the teams know that they can cancel those weekend plans. The way this is done is that the selected team is herded into a compartment or room, the area is secured, the doors are closed, and somebody, normally the unit commander, will issue a Warning Order.

In various forms, warning orders have been around since the Mongol hordes, since Attila, since Alexander the Great. In its short form it sounds something like, "We're going to break camp in the morning before sunrise and attack the infidels, sack their town, rape their women, and put the place to the torch. Bring your sword, spear, and all your armor. Questions?"

The modern version is more complicated, but the idea is identical. It gives the people involved an idea, usually incomplete, of what they are going to be doing and what they should do to prepare. The formal version (used by the Army and Marines as well) includes a brief description of the situation; the mission; general instructions, including organization, uniform, weapons, chain of command, schedule, including time for the more detailed patrol order, and for inspections and rehearsals; and specific instructions for subordinate leaders and individuals.

Everybody then scurries around, collecting weapons, demolition material, MREs, fresh batteries for the radios, and night vision goggles. *Nobody* gets to call home and say, "Guess

69

what, Honey, I'm not gonna be home on time tonight 'cause we're off to defend freedom and democracy . . . "

Instead, they just don't come home in the evening. Sooner or later the families might get some extremely vague information, but that's one of the costs of admission to the special op-

Although they wear the same uniforms and carry the same weapons as other US forces, SEALs are unique in their combination of talents and tasking. SEALs train and fight in extremely small units with missions in or around the water. These missions may be to support either a Navy boss or a joint theater boss who could be an Army, Air Force, or Marine officer. They may be extremely covert, or extremely unconventional. Regardless, the basic weapon of Naval Special Warfare isn't the rifle but the man behind it, and the tiny team of which he is a part.

erations and rapid-deployment military communities. And not only do these call-ups happen for real world events, they are called for training, too, with irregular frequency.

The idea behind the Warning Order is that, once the order comes down to the unit, a fixed amount of time will be specified before the operation is supposed to be executed—perhaps twelve hours. The platoon or squad leader is expected to take a third of that time to make his own preliminary plan, and allocate two-thirds of the time to the subordinates to do their preparation and rehearsals. While it often doesn't work out that neatly, the idea is a sound one and is applied as much as circumstances permit.

SOPs

Each platoon has its own set of Standard Operating Procedures, its own identity, its unique reputation and subculture, all based somewhat on the characters on the team.

SOPs make planning and executing operations far faster and more efficient than otherwise. When a Patrol Leader's Order is issued only the unique details of the mission need to be discussed—radio frequencies, rendezvous points, routes in and out of the objective, commander's intent. All the other essentials—patrol order of march, actions on contact, reaction to ambush, individual responsibilities— all these things have been long since memorized as a kind of "company policy" that doesn't need repeating. Most of the members of the teams, like Bob Gormly's SEAL Team Two, had known each other for four or five years and could just about execute an operation without a word ever being spoken.

Patrol Leader's Order

The five-paragraph format used to formally brief the mission has been in use since World War I, its format memorized by millions of servicemen over the years. It forces the unit to plan logically to deal with an extremely stressful and dangerous experience. The elements of the order are the situation, the mission, the details of the execution, how the mis-

When SEALs jump, the rubber duck goes out first, followed promptly by the SEALs. The hard part is hustling out of the aircraft with those darn fins on.

sion will be supported and supplied, and command and communications. Depending on the complexity of the mission, the Orders Brief can last a few minutes or six hours; an hour or so is typical. SEALs may get some of the most difficult and dangerous missions, but they also get some of the very best and most expensive intelligence support, often custom-made for the specific mission. This will almost always include "overhead" imagery, photographs from all altitudes, from low level all the way up to the secret satellites like the KA-11. There may be radio and telephone intercepts, and reports from agents in the operations area. And (in extreme and rare cases) a prisoner may be snatched out of the target area, brought back to chat with the team, and held until the mis-

sion concludes and the team is safely extracted.

SEALs like to rehearse their missions, and if it is practical to do so, some kind of run-through will be done. This might be no more than a detailed brainstorming conference somewhere in the bowels of a submarine, or it might involve the construction of a mock-up of a target and a complete rehearsal of the entire mission ashore. Regardless, once the Patrol Leader's Order has been given, none of the players will be going anywhere or doing anything except preparing to launch into the op area.

When it is time to go to work, SEALs commute in dramatic and dangerous ways. Although trained for insertion to an operating

Water parachute landings are potentially treacherous, particularly at night. The MC-1 canopy used by this jumper is steerable and has a moderate forward speed. Now, about a hundred feet above the water, the jumper should be facing into the wind, chest band and reserve unfastened, reserve parachute shoved to the side. Assume a good prepare-to-land position: head up, eyes on the horizon, knees bent. US Navy photo

area by parachute, that's really not the SEALs' forte. Except in rare instances, the mission will begin with an insertion over or under the surface of the water.

At any time there are SEALs deployed aboard US submarines operating around the world, waiting for world events to call for their

services. When the orders trickle down the chain of command, the SEALs plan their mission and use the most stealthy technique of all to drop in on the enemy—submarine insertion.

US subs have a small chamber, the "escape trunk," installed forward of the sail. This little chamber has two functions, the first allowing for trapped submariners to escape a boat sunken in shallow water, and the second (a secondary use) allowing for the deployment and recovery of combat swimmers.

Locking out of a sub is not for the faint of heart. The swimmers don their wet suits and their combat equipment, collect weapons, explosives, and related equipment, and prepare to enter the chamber; scuba or Draeger rigs are, believe it or not, optional. Then, one after another, they climb into the chamber, a spherical space about six feet across. Up to five combat swimmers can crowd into the chamber, but all will be extremely cramped and uncomfortable. Even among trained and experienced SEALs panic sometimes occurs as the water is slowly allowed in. There are mouthpieces and air lines installed in the chamber, and it is possible to use the sub's own air supply for breathing until the chamber is unlocked and it is time to leave. But SEALs normally use their own rigs—if they have any. It is quite possible to ascend to the surface without scuba or rebreather, and SEALs train for this "free ascent" or "blow and go" technique—as well as the reverse technique required to come back aboard.

The sub will slither in as close to shore as the skipper and the SEALs can agree on. Subs are not normally content to be in shallow water close to a hostile coast; SEALs are normally not pleased to swim in from over the horizon. So the typical mission will bring the SSN attack sub into a mile or two off the coast on a dark and hopefully stormy night. The sub

Here's another way to get to work—a Swimmer Delivery Vehicle being deployed by a submerged submarine. The SDV is kind of a submarine itself, although its passengers get cold and wet. US Navy photo

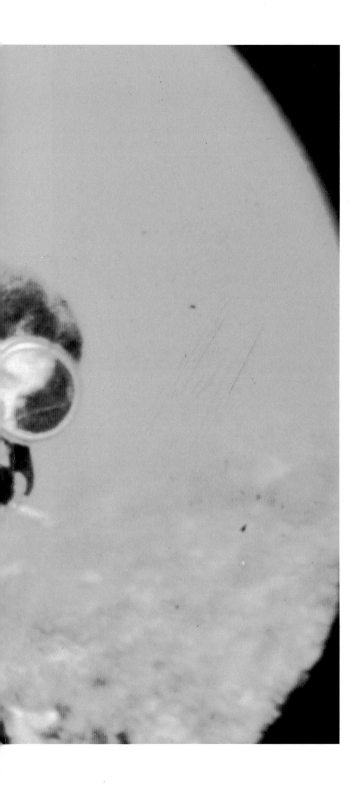

will come up to a depth of about forty feet, bring the periscope up for a quick peek at the neighborhood, then bring it back down. The 'scope makes a fair radar reflector, and if somebody is working a surface search radar tweaked for such targets, there could be a problem. So the sub crew gets extremely edgy about this kind of mission.

A typical insertion out of the chamber will have one man go out first, with scuba, and rig the Zodiac stored in the sail locker on deck. The boat will have to be taken to the surface while a tether is left attached to the submarine. This entire complex activity is done in darkness, almost entirely by touch, and takes about half an hour. When the diver has the boat properly infiltrated and on a tow, he signals the sub to send up the rest of the SEALs. Even this isn't quick or easy: he can flash a light signal at the periscope if the sub skipper is willing to raise it, he can swim down and rap on the hull, or he can even go back in the lockout chamber, repressurize and have a chat via microphone.

Usually, though, a simple rap on the hull will do it. Then the next batch of divers cram into the chamber, the water level rises, and finally somebody has to wriggle a hand over to the valves and latches that will open the hatch.

"You get into there, you've got all this weight on you, you close the bottom hatch, you stand there, doubled over—tanks on your back, equipment in your arms—three to five people jammed in there. Then somebody has to find a way to reach over to the valve so you can start to flood the chamber. There are some guys who are just more nervous about all this—everybody jammed in that small space, water coming up to your neck. I've seen guys panic in there."

It takes a long time, usually in cold, high seas, for the seven or eight men to rig the boats and exit the sub for a typical mission of

Locking out of a sub involves swimming out of a little chamber about the size of the hatch visible in this shot. US Navy photo

The M60 machine gun puts serious suppressive fire downrange. The M60 is an area weapon, used for delivering a heavy volume of fire at a distance.

this type. Hypothermia and seasickness will be a problem for those already in the boat up on the surface while the nervousness of the sub crew will be a problem for those still aboard. Even the rubber boats have a radar return signature, and if anybody is looking, the whole operation can suddenly become a target instead of a weapon. It is a very nervous time. But then, after perhaps a couple of hours, you're all set and its time to go ashore.

Dry Deck Shelter

There is an easier way, a bolt-on chamber that is called the Dry Deck Shelter (DDS). While it operates on the same principle as the lock-out chamber, it is far larger. The DDS is big enough to accommodate a whole platoon, with dive gear and rubber boats, radios and demolitions. It will also accommodate the Swimmer Deliver Vehicle, the SEAL-scooter

that is designed for zipping around underwater. Besides these handy features, it converts to a hyperbaric chamber for treating a diver who's been "bent" from staying under too long, too deep, and acquires the painful, potentially fatal condition called "decompression sickness."

While the general insertion technique for the DDS is the same as with the lock-out chamber, it is a lot faster and a lot less crowded. The whole evolution goes faster, much to the delight of the submarine crew.

To the Beach

Once everybody's safely in a Zodiak, it's time to break out the paddles or fire up the engine and head to the beach. Several hundred meters offshore, well outside the surf zone, a pair of divers—the scout swimmers—will slip over the gunwales of the Zodiac and, with weapons at the ready, move in to secure the section of beach where the landing is intended. After a quick check of the area, they signal the boats to come in. The "rubber ducks" run in through the surf, everybody alert for enemy contact, and the boats are promptly pulled up across the high water mark and either hidden or buried.

Once secure on the beach, the SEALs are ready to execute the mission. If it is a patrol or a "direct action" strike deep inland, the squad (or perhaps platoon if two boats have come ashore) assembles itself and prepares to move off into the hinterland without a word being spoken. Communication is done with hand and arm signals, visible and instantly recognizable even on dark, cloudy nights.

Out front, leading the patrol, is the point man who navigates the patrol to the objective. This is traditionally the most dangerous, difficult position in the patrol order, requiring superb land navigation skills and an extremely high level of alertness to the possibility of contact with enemy forces. A point man can walk you right into the kill zone of an ambush, or halt the patrol safely outside. Such choices can be (and often have been) the difference of life and death for an entire patrol. When contact with the enemy is made, the man on point is typically the first to fire or the first to die.

The point man's preferred weapon in wooded terrain is often not a rifle or machine gun but a military version of a standard twelve-gauge shotgun, loaded with five rounds of "double-ought" (size 00) buckshot. These are large, bullet-sized lead pellets that spread out in a lethal cone of destruction. One pellet will kill out to a range of about 100 meters, sometimes farther; at closer ranges, particularly within about ten meters, a well-placed load will punch a gaping hole through a torso, or rip off an arm or a head. It is the approximate equivalent of firing seven or so bullets at exactly the same instant in the same general direction.

An alternative load is the flachette round, with tiny steel darts in place of the buckshot. While these are not nearly as lethal or de-

structive individually, there are many more of them, and they produce a denser cloud of projectiles, a handy way of providing a group of enemy soldiers at close range with something to think about besides the SEAL patrol. They are lethal out to several hundred meters.

There's yet another handy twelve-gauge round for the point man's shotgun, a single, heavy slug useful for opening locked doors and disabling machinery or electronics in one quick, brutal way. It is accurate out to a range of about five feet, maybe six. If it hits some-

The M16 coupled with the M203 grenade launcher is a potent combination used to engage point targets out to about a quarter of a mile. The collapsible stock and short barrel make the weapon less awkward to get in and out of cramped places like lockout chambers.

This sentry doesn't know it but he's got a little problem. That's an invisible infrared aim-point dot on his personal center-of-mass. Since the aiming device is attached to a rifle, that means the bullets from the weapon will strike within that dot, probably creating some discomfort for the target.

thing, the target stays hit. This is no precision munition, but it will punch a hole in the cast-iron block of an automobile engine, or the concrete wall of a house or bunker—or, if they co-operate, a whole row of enemy soldiers.

Riflemen

If the point man bumps into a bad guy at close range and gets the first shot off effectively, the patrol has the choice of either "going to ground" and duking it out with the opposing team or making a run for the beach. In either case the point man's shotgun will soon have limited utility—it will be out of range, out of ammunition, or both. That's why there are several riflemen on a normal patrol, each with an M16 rifle and five or six thirty-round magazines stashed in their load-carrying web gear.

M16A2 and Car-15

The M16A2 rifle is almost the same weapon that the father's of some of today's SEALs carried and fought with in Vietnam a generation ago. It's no longer the most exotic weapon on the battlefield, or on the teams, but it is still a good, light, accurate, effective weapon that has proven itself in countless battles. The latest version is more reliable than the first, which had a failure-to-feed problem for a while. The A2 also lacks the "full-auto" feature of the original, a modification based on the discovery that in the heat of combat the weapon was being used as a "bullet hose," ineffectively spraying rounds downrange. Instead, the rifle has a BURST position on the selector switch on the left side of the receiver, above the trigger; this permits three-round bursts that economize on ammunition while encouraging the rifleman to aim rather than point the weapon.

While the basic rifle issued to SEALs is essentially the same as the M16A2 issued to Army and Marine Corps infantry privates (and just about everybody else, too), the SEALs version tends to be an upgraded, customized weapon with specialized sights and a collapsible stock or a compact version of the

The little MP5 "room broom" is a super-compact little squirt gun that's a favorite of SEALs and other *operators who have to deal face to face with terrorists at short range.*

M16 that has been popular with special operators for the last twenty years, the CAR-15. This little squirt gun uses essentially the same receiver components as the bigger M16, but with an ingenious collapsible stock assembly and shorter barrel. It trades bulk for a little fragility and a slightly greater inclination to jam. The decision to carry the CAR-15 or M16 is—as with similar decisions on a team—partly a matter of personal choice. SEALs, along with other special operators, are permitted to exercise a lot more latitude in the choice of accessories than are troopers in more conventional units.

Depending on the particular mission, the sights installed may be a night-vision scope or a laser aim-point system. The first of these, the night-vision scope, amplifies existing light and presents the shooter with a magnified, green and black picture of the target through a somewhat conventional rifle scope. The other device mounts a small laser pointer under the barrel; once activated it puts a bright red dot where the bullet will strike. You

don't need to peep through a scope or iron sights—just put the red dot on your intended victim and squeeze. It is not a long-range, sniping system; but for night combat in confined spaces it is often the system of choice.

The M16 fires a small, 5.56mm (.223-caliber) bullet at high velocity. This makes for a very flat trajectory and a lot of retained energy at practical ranges. The Vietnam-era version of the M16 was supposed to be good out to about 300 meters; today's weapon/cartridge combination is rated to 460 meters—about a quarter of a mile. That means that a trained rifleman can hit a man-sized target at that range with about fifty percent of his carefully aimed shots. The bullet, of course, is lethal out to a couple of miles, but hitting things with it at extreme ranges has more to do with luck than gun control.

MP4 and MP5

The M16 and CAR-15 are not the only choices for a SEAL rifleman to take on a mission. His weapon can be almost anything that he and the patrol leader think is appropriate.

One favorite alternative is the Heckler & Koch (H&K) MP5 "room broom" submachine gun. It fires the diminutive 9mm Parabellum pistol round and is well matched to the laser aimpoint sight system for urban combat situations. It is extremely compact—you can wear it under a jacket for those formal events. Like the shotgun, it is accurate and effective only out to fifty meters or so, and its projectiles aren't guaranteed to have the desired effect. But you can carry (and shoot) a lot of those little 9mm rounds; if you squirt a burst of them into a bunker the folks inside will probably wish you hadn't.

The bigger brother of the MP5 is a beefy submachine gun called the MP4 , brought to you by those fine folks at H&K, builders of fine military weapons used around the world. Both of these German weapons possess a qual-ity that, in many ways, is more important than accuracy, hitting power, weight or rate of fire: when you pull the trigger the gun goes *bang*. This reputation for reliability has sold a lot of H&K weapons to a lot of operators, and it is the reason you'll so often see them, dripping sea water and covered with sand, coming across a beach in the hands of SEALs.

Silencers

On the muzzles of all these rifles and submachine guns you'll sometimes see tubular devices about eight inches long and an inch and a half in diameter. These are sound suppressers, or silencers as they are sometimes called. For weapons such as the 9mm H&Ks, with subsonic ammunition, they can convert the loud report to a subtle pop by slowing the propellant gasses as they rush out the muzzle behind the bullet. This can be a very handy

The MP4 is very popular with the teams, and rightfully so. It is compact, reliable, and tolerant of saltwater immersion. Its little 9mm round isn't the *hardest hitting bullet on the block, but it works well enough at close range.*

80

feature in those sneaky, close-in fights that SEALs sometimes encounter.

Suppressers work on the M16, too, but not nearly as well. The standard ammunition for the weapon is designed to produce very high velocities, far faster than the speed of sound. Much of the noise from the firing of an M16 comes from the sonic boom produced by the bullet's flight through air. Even so, some of the noise can be reduced, and suppressers are often attached even to M16s, particularly in urban combat situations. As with the aimpoint and night sights and so many other tools of the trade, suppressers have their specialized role in the SEALs' bag of tricks.

M203 Grenade Launcher

One of the most interesting and useful weapons you'll find carried on a SEAL mission is the M203 grenade launcher, a fairly simple weapon with a complex variety of ammunition and uses. It isn't much more than a short length of aluminum tube with a breech block and trigger assembly. It bolts to an M16 rifle, under the barrel; the magazine provides the hand grip. The 203 fires a 40mm cartridge with one of several warheads. It is a bit like a mortar, although it is called a grenade launcher. Its lobbing trajectory allows you to toss projectiles over berms and other forms of cover that your opponent may use to hide from direct fire weapons. Within about two or three hundred meters you should, with training, be able to put one of the rounds through a doorway or bunker aperture (although it might take a few tries).

Projectiles come in several flavors. There is a high explosive model (HE) that is one of the most popular. It will reach out about 500

The M203 grenade launcher throws a 40mm projectile out several hundred yards with precision. It's not much more than a simple aluminum tube with a breech and trigger. The hand grip is the rifle's magazine. With it, you can pump a few anti-personnel rounds through the aperture of a bunker, or an illumination round up in the air, or an anti-armor round into the side of an armored personnel carrier, normally with the desired results.

81

In conventional units the automatic weapons man gets an assistant to feed the ammunition. SEALs manage this chore themselves. The orange bullet tip indicates a tracer round; the others are ball.

Another view of the M203. It's not much more than a simple aluminum tube with a breech and trigger. The hand grip is the rifle's magazine.

Combat Time

Although Naval Special Warfare represents some of the best trained, most experienced warriors in the US Department of Defense, there is still something just a little naive about the vast majority of the people in this community. While they train to the highest standards and with the most realistic training aids, there is still something missing from the resumes of nearly all the 1,200 SEALs and SBS crews today: combat time.

About twenty years have now passed since the end of America's last prolonged conflict. With those years have gradually gone the SEALs who planned and executed the missions in the Mekong during the long, difficult years the teams fought in Vietnam. The result of that is that, in some ways, the teams are becoming *less* qualified rather than more so as time goes by. The lessons learned from prolonged combat operations in what military folks call the "real world" cannot be duplicated in peacetime. Now, when SEALs go to war, it is typically the first real combat operation of a career, and perhaps the only combat experience a man will ever have. Of the 200-plus men on one of today's teams, there is probably not one left with Vietnam experience, and very, very few with actual trigger-pulling experience in any operation since.

Real combat makes people do things they don't do in training. The big, heroic guys sometimes go numb and ineffective on you while the wimpy little guys who always screw up during training execute the mission with calm and grace and not a trace of fear.

In training you shoot at a cardboard or plastic target that pops up for a few mechanically timed seconds, usually in a predictable place, then disappears. If you hit it, the target folds down, mechanically, and a computer records your hit. In combat your target will appear anywhere, often unpredictably, often for a fraction of a second. The target may be a woman or a child, may be trying to shoot you, or may not know you exist. You can see its eyes, sometimes; you can identify it as a person, somewhat like you. The target probably has a family, a mission of his own, and maybe a target of his own—you. It is a bit like hunting; you must expect the unexpected, be alert without fixation, all in a complicated, emotional, supremely frightening situation. When your target appears, it will probably be for a fleeting glimpse. If you are completely prepared, you may be able to get a shot off. If you do, you will certainly invite the same treatment on yourself.

Things they don't show you on television:

No matter how well you've maintained your weapon, no matter how full the magazine is or how carefully it has been loaded, there will be times when you pull the trigger on somebody and it will go *click* instead of *bang*. This can be quite embarrassing. It happens a lot more often than you can possibly imagine.

Gunfights on TV and in the movies are fought with weapons that have magical, bottomless magazines, that never run out of ammunition. Real world gunfights use weapons with magazines that are good for about three seconds full-auto, less if they jam (which they often will). And magazines that you can easily change in training, at night and with gloves on, you will find yourself utterly incapable of fitting into the well of the weapon. You will run out of ammunition far faster than you could imagine possible.

In a real world gunfight you can spot a target, align the sights, cut loose with a long burst from your trusty M60, and watch the tracers dance downrange at the man you intend to kill, when, just like in the movies, the dust kicks up around him, the bullets hammer his surroundings—and he runs off, untouched.

But if you somehow achieve that Zen-like state of mind that some men do, all things are possible. An enemy soldier can materialize out of the weeds, with your personal weapon jammed or broken, and now it is *his* turn to forget in nervous haste to move the safety on his AK-74 from "safe" to "fire." Then, perhaps, you will remember why you carry that Sig-Sauer 9mm handgun on your hip. If you get to the Sig quick enough, get it up, focus on the front sight, align with center-of-mass, and squeeze—if you are blessed this day—your bullet will strike your man in the lower sternum. He'll go down, and you can stay up; you'll live through another mission. If you're lucky and good, together.

None of these things will ever happen to you on an exercise or in training, but they will all happen to you if you go to war with a combat unit and stay there awhile. Trust me on this.

meters and will kill or injure anybody within about five meters of impact, a useful device when enemy infantry are closing in on your position. The 203 will also fire illumination rounds, like the mortar, that will light up the battlefield at night; and tear gas, white phosphorus, and flachette rounds for other times and places.

M60 Machine Gun

A SEAL squad with an inland patrol mission will carry plenty of "organic" firepower in the form of two stripped down M60 machine guns. The M60 is another old design that has been improved since the years when the dad of today's SEAL carried one back in the "big war." It fires the bigger 7.62mm (.308-caliber) NATO cartridge, delivering accurate, high-volume fire on area targets at ranges well beyond what the M16 can effectively engage.

It is a heavy weapon, with heavy ammunition, often cursed on those long walks in the woods and swamps—until, that is, the opposing team materializes out of the woodwork, spoiling for a fight. Then the M60 is worth its weight in gold or blood.

If this seems like a lot of choices, it is. A team commander explains his personal attitude toward weapons used by SEALs:

"I think we really do need a variety of weapons on the teams. Certain operations call for specific capabilities. I also don't think every guy should have a different weapon, just because he has his own personal preference. I should be able to switch magazines with the guy next to me if I run out and he hasn't. But, for the rifleman, the choice can be between the M14, the MP5, or the M16. The MP5 is for use in brush or urban combat situations. The M16 is a good, general, all-around weapon, and you can put the M203 under it. The M14 has extra power for penetration and range.

"Riflemen are for engaging *point* targets and they should be shooting single shots; personally, I don't even believe in three-round bursts. I don't even believe in 'double-tap' [firing two quick shots at a target instead of one], although the idea is currently quite popular. If you put the first shot where you're supposed

The M60 as used by the SEALs is a stripped-down, lightweight version that is a lot more tolerant of sand than the early versions were. After firing a hundred rounds or so the barrel will begin to glow.

to, you don't *need* another one! If you need another one, pull the trigger again. Why waste ammunition? You should be calm enough under fire to know what you are doing rather than just opening up 'full-auto' and spraying the riverbank.

"The automatic weapon man is not to take out point targets; he's supposed to keep the enemy's head down and to give you covering fire while the riflemen take care of the point targets."

RTO

The patrol can be far from a friendly face but still be in contact with the civilized world, thanks to the battery-powered high technology that the RTO (an old expression, short for radio telephone operator) carries. There are any number of systems he can carry, and with some of them you can chat with the big bosses

The RTO is the squad communicator. His duties include carrying the radio and batteries and managing the communications plan. The antenna will identify him as a prime target to any enemy snipers within rifle range.

you can call for help from almost anywhere on the globe with these little systems, if some politician in the "puzzle palace" comes up with a wild hair idea, they can call *you* and task you with this death-defying scheme, all from the comfort and safety of Washington, DC.

The RTO is, in some ways, a pack mule for the patrol leader; he carries the radio and operates it, but under the control of the patrol leader, whom the RTO shadows. The RTO is, along with the officer, a natural target for any sensible sniper on the opposing team who manages to identify and engage the patrol. The radio is the patrol's link to the close air support gunships overhead, the naval gunfire support offshore, and the "slicks" (unarmed helicopters) ready to swoop in to rescue the patrol in an emergency. By eliminating the RTO and his equipment, the enemy can isolate the squad and chop it to small pieces. That's why RTOs fold the aerials of their radios down and do their best to look as innocent as possible.

A funny thing about these radios, though, is that—despite their usually excellent reliability and reception—at moments like these they may suddenly stop working. As one officer explains:

"We have better communications now than we used to, but that works both ways. If I need to get ahold of somebody I probably can. It also means that guy can get ahold of me—and give me directions that I might not want. I can remember two times, during 1965 operations in Vietnam, when somebody tried to tell me what to do while I was on the ground. I didn't like it—and in one case I turned off the radio. Now, if the National Command Authority wants to talk to me while I'm on a hot operation, they very well may. This is not necessarily a good thing. To me, the guy on the scene calls the shots. He should receive *nothing* from those guys except support, when he calls up and asks for it. We make a plan and should stick to the plan, unless the guy on the ground wants to do differently. Now, if somebody has some information that can help you, if they see a platoon of enemy, for example,

in Washington and in the Pentagon—although that's not usually something the team will think is a good idea.

That's because you're on the ground, with eyes on the target, and the admirals and the assistant secretary of defense sitting next to him are both in a comfortable room in a safe place. When the sun goes down, they will go off for cocktails somewhere, have a nice dinner, and watch TV. You will crawl through the mud and perhaps have people shoot at you, all while attempting to do the bidding of these "experts" with the clean fingernails, thanks to that little "satcom" transceiver carried by the RTO.

Satellite radios are now extremely compact and can easily be taken along on operations with a very moderate weight penalty. They allow the team leader to communicate with almost anybody, almost anywhere (if he can get a channel on the satellite). That, believe it or not, can be a real problem. Although

coming down the road toward you, they ought to be able to let you know. But don't tell me to go left or right in reaction to that platoon—let *me* make that decision!

"We have a tendency, because we have such good communications, to let responsibility slip upwards where sometimes it doesn't belong. Look what happened at Desert One [the failed Iranian hostage rescue mission]. Jimmy Carter was in the position where he could call up Colonel Beckwith [the on-scene commander] and tell him what to do. I don't like that! Most people in the SEALs don't like that. Some people submit to that. And some people automatically get their hackles up—don't submit to it; put the radio down and say 'Dang, something just went wrong with the radio!' The problem with letting decisions be made someplace, with letting somebody else be re-

PRC-112 squad radio is another example in the revolution in miniaturization that has transformed the command and control problem for managing SEALs during combat operations.

sponsible, is that I'm still responsible for the people who are with me. I want to make the decision for what happens once we launch the mission. Tell me what to do *before* I leave, and then if I buy off on it, fine. Just don't tell me what to do once I'm out there. While we have the advantage of better communications, we get with that the disadvantage of potential micro-management by people not on the scene."

Patrol Leader

The patrol leader on a SEAL operation is going to be one of the platoon's two commissioned officers, the platoon leader (normally a lieutenant) or executive officer (lieutenant junior grade or possibly ensign). The role of a combat leader is an odd kind of combination of duties that sometimes conflict. A combat leader has two heavy responsibilities: to complete the mission, and to preserve the force. That means that the leader takes himself and his followers to complete a mission that, in war, will probably involve great hazard. How much hazard is sometimes influenced by the officer; it may depend on how much risk he's willing to take in a given time and place. Just how important the mission is he has to judge. He has to judge how much it is worth, in time, effort, ammunition, and the blood of his men. So the patrol leader is stuck in the middle, with a responsibility upward, to his commanders who've tasked him with a mission, and downward, to his followers who trust his judgment.

The officer is part of the platoon, and he is aloof from it. He guards his men, is responsible for their welfare as a parent is for a child—and may send them knowingly to their deaths or dismemberment. He is trained, at Annapolis or OCS (Officer Candidate School), to be careful to avoid playing favorites and developing the natural kind of friendships that are common among civilians—fraternization, it is called.

The officer discovers, early in his career, that while the troops will automatically salute and call him *sir*, the respect may not be sincere. An officer learns that respect is earned in two phases: first through the commissioning process that awards gold bars and officer rank, then all over again in the units where real competence and leadership are demonstrated. For SEALs there is another part, BUD/S, where officers must perform alongside the enlisted sailors, suffer all the same insults and indignities, the same stresses and fatigue. It is an important part of the bonding between the leaders and the followers in the SEALs.

As officer candidates quickly learn at Annapolis, NROTC, or OCS, it's a complicated business to lead men in combat. It is a bit like leading an orchestra; you don't need to be the best player of every instrument, but you have to know perfectly what each can do—then to be able to make sure its resources are integrated into the big score. But the terrible,

This is one of the little compact SATCOM radios that have transformed the business of communicating in the field. This is the LST-5C transceiver; it weighs about ten pounds.

wonderful thing about military operations is that they are, always and invariably, partially improvisations. There is an old military saying: No plan survives contact with the enemy. That means that, no matter how well you think you've prepared, something is going to go wrong. And when it does, one person needs to be responsible for selecting an alternative course of action. That's what officers are for.

The platoon leader will normally have been personally given the mission and then designed the plan, with help from above and below. He takes the plan to the field and makes it happen with the help of his SEALs. When the shooting starts he is expected to direct, manage, and control the firing. When the ambush is triggered, he initiates it with a squeeze of the trigger or the "clacker" for the Claymore. His M16 magazines may be full of nothing but tracers, which he uses to indicate targets for the rest of the squad to fire on.

On the march, the patrol leader will typically be toward the front of the line of march. He may take the point sometimes, but usually will be the number two man, where he can provide direction for the man on point and still control the squad in case of contact. The RTO will be right behind the patrol leader, however, wherever he is.

Tail Gunner

The two most vulnerable areas for the patrol are its front and its back; it will either bump into trouble, or trouble will come sneaking up on it. That's why both the man on point and the last man in line, the tail gunner, have to be especially sharp. The tail gunner will probably have one of the squad's cut-down M60 machine guns—and eyes in the back of his head.

In actual combat, on deep penetration missions, he'll probably carry a variety of goodies to help break contact if the patrol finds itself compromised and on the run. Then he'll pull out the tear gas grenades, the devastating WP (white phosphorous) grenades, and perhaps a Claymore to rig as a booby trap against the pursuers.

Chapter 5

Actions at the Objective

As mentioned before, SEALs have five different general types of missions to perform: direct action, recon, foreign internal defense, unconventional warfare, and counterterrorist. This is a broad spectrum of responsibilities for a small organization, no matter how well trained or funded. Some of these are primary SEAL missions; others are secondary.

Counterterrorist operations, for example, are really the stock-in-trade for Delta, the Army's superb, extremely exclusive counterterrorist unit. The men (and—promise not to tell where you heard this—women) in Delta are going to get the call for such operations except under extreme circumstances. SEALs are trained and prepared to execute the operation, and there are a few "long hair" team members available for extremely covert ops, but it is hardly a prime talent for aquatic warriors.

Likewise, foreign internal defense (FID) and unconventional warfare (UW) are prime Army missions that are backed up by SEALs. Both require the language skills and charm of a diplomat, the charisma of an evangelist, and the patience of a saint. The FID mission turns out to be one that a few SEALs excel at, about five guys of the 200 or so on a team, according to one team commander. This mission occupies a few SEALs in Latin America now, and it kept a lot busy during the workup to Desert Storm in training Saudi and other Arab naval personnel in the Gulf. As one of the team commanders says:

"I think we're quite good at the traditional Green Beret mission of foreign internal defense; we have a very high degree of success when we include foreign military personnel in our operations. For some reason we've thrown that back to the Army. We were very good in the Gulf when we took two or three SEALs and used them with ten or twelve host-nation personnel. We 'force-multiplied.' We had all the advantages of the host-nation expertise, plus our skills and experience in executing that type of operation. It was a Cracker Jack setup!"

But it is not one most SEALs find very appealing. It takes many months of study at DLI, the Defense Language Institute at Monterey, California, to acquire the skill to speak Arabic, for example, or Estonian, and that means time away from the teams. Unconventional warfare is the behind-the-lines version of FID, and hasn't really been used much since World War II—although it is still sitting there as a tasking for the Special Operations Forces.

So the principal missions, the ones that get the attention, the time, the rehearsals, are

When you're a SEAL you don't have to worry too much about what the sign says, particularly when you've got a riot shotgun and an MP4. Close combat in confined spaces is a new skill required of SEALs. US Navy photo by PH2 Milton Savage

recon and strike. The first is stealthy and the second isn't.

Recons, Deep and Shallow

Despite all the wonderful, expensive technology that has gone into intelligence gathering, with billions of dollars spent on camera systems for aircraft and satellites, there is still no substitute for having someone go ashore for a "hands on, eyes on" study of a potential target. One of the lessons learned from Urgent

The SPIE (Special Purpose Insertion and Extraction) rig is one way to extract and insert SEALs in a hurry. It is a breezy and hazardous technique, but one that a lot of people actually enjoy. US Navy photo by PH2 Milton Savage

Fury was that overhead intel only begins to provide essential planning information and that things like landing zones can look completely different to a helicopter pilot than to a high-flying aircraft—with potentially catastrophic results.

Although not as glamorous as the strike missions, recon ops are just as important now as ever. As the recons in the Panama Just Cause op and the beach survey during Desert Storm both demonstrate, SEALs still get tasked with these jobs, and it is their particular art form.

The recon mission can be just about anything, anywhere. The classic one, of course, is the beach recon preceding an amphibious operation. While the Marines think their own recon guys can do this better than anybody, SEALs politely disagree. While it doesn't get much attention, it is still a tremendously important mission when you consider how much investment the US has in putting Marines across the beach anywhere in the world. The memory of Tarawa half a century ago haunts the Marines—and the Navy, too. Beach recons, consequently, are a big part of the course of instruction at BUD/S, where they're called "hydrographic surveys." They can be as simple or as detailed as you and your commanders want—and as circumstances permit.

There are many different types of hydrographic surveys and beach recons, from simple to complex. The amphibious task force commander who is planning an across-the-beach op will want to know gradient and composition of the beach, littoral current across the beach, surf size and type, beach exits, defenses, and obstacles underwater.

It takes a lot of people—or a lot of time—to develop this information. Without getting into the technical details, here's how they do it:

Swim pairs are dropped in the water off the beach at intervals of about twenty-five meters, on line, by a high-speed boat—just like they did fifty years ago out in the Pacific. Under command of the officer in charge (OIC), the swimmers move in toward the beach, mak-

A fire team (half a squad) fits neatly into a rubber duck for a semi-stealthy insertion. Although the little inflatable is rated for over-the-horizon ranges, you don't want to ride around like this for long out on the open ocean.

First ashore during a combat insertion are the scout swimmers, who secure the beach before the rest of the unit comes ashore. They operate in pairs, for mutual security.

ing soundings with a lead-line (a lead sinker on a line marked in one-foot increments). While one man measures the depth, the other records the data on a slate. Since all the swimmers make these soundings at the same time, a set of coordinated data is assembled across a wide frontage of possible landing zone.

The line of swimmers moves in to the beach together, with the OIC controlling the intervals between soundings. Both depth and composition are recorded on each swim-pair's slate. The Marine task force commander's staff will want to know what they have to contend with. Coral reef? Mud? Jagged rocks? Man-made obstacles with antitank mines attached? Is the foreshore (the surf zone) too shallow for LSTs, or is it steep and suitable for ramped vessels? Is the surf high and violent or short and mild? Is the current across the beach strong and likely to force the AAM-TRACs away from their intended beaches? Then, what's beyond the beach—will tanks and armored vehicles be "channeled" by sea walls, cliffs, embankments? Are there enemy-prepared fighting positions dominating the beach? Are they manned? Is there a beach patrol? Are there mines?

The survey party moves all the way into the beach and perhaps beyond, then withdraws back to the water. Under the direction of the OIC, they reform a line offshore for pickup. Then, perhaps aboard the flagship for the amphibious task force or wherever the SEAL unit has set up shop, the data from each swim pair is assembled as a detailed chart and presented to the plans-and-operations guys who are trying to figure out what to do. They (through their recommendation to the task force commander) make the call on the amphibious operation, not the SEALs, using the data provided.

There is another kind of recon for which the Army and Navy SOF communities compete, called *deep recon* or *strategic recon*, and this one might not involve even getting wet. Deep recon involves the study of a target or area of interest that typically requires covert travel overland or covert insertion inland. SOF teams did this during Desert Shield/Desert Storm in Kuwait and Iraq, watching for enemy SCUD launchers, for example, and reporting their location for attack by other "theater assets" like US Air Force F-15E Strike Eagle aircraft. A SEAL recon team was on the Saudi/Kuwait border when the Iraqis attacked the town of Kafji and participated in the coordinated engagement of the enemy armored column by air and coalition ground units.

HAHO and HALO Insertion

These recon teams can be delivered in some quite exotic ways. One of the sneakiest is by parachute, but SOF teams don't consider the standard 500- or 1,200-foot drop altitude used for mass tactical airborne operations to be very covert; having a C-130 fly low over the neighborhood is one sure way to get noticed. Instead, the drop aircraft goes way up to 30,000 feet or so—where the commercial airliners fly. The jumpers, rigged with special equipment to cope with the incredible cold and the lack of oxygen at that altitude, jump and free fall before deploying their canopies.

The HAHO technique (High-Altitude exit/High-altitude Opening) allows a jumper to glide for many miles under his canopy, through the dark, virtually without fear of detection, to a predetermined landing zone.

The HALO technique (High-Altitude exit/Low-altitude Opening) is a similar way to have the jumper move away from the ground track of the aircraft, making it difficult to find him. This time, though, the jumper uses freefall parachuting techniques to "fly" through the air, opening his canopy only when very close to the ground.

Once down, the mission proceeds as planned. When it is over, one way or another, it is time to go home. While, again, there are many ways to do this, the quickest will again be by aircraft. Unfortunately, though, pickup aircraft are a lot less subtle.

STABO Extraction

An extremely unsubtle extraction technique, STABO (Stabilized Tactical Airborne Body Operations), involves having a helicopter arrive over the team on the ground with a special harness deployed, coming to a hover, and then plucking the SEALs out of harm's way. The SEALs all wear harnesses similar to those used for parachuting and attach the harnesses to the sling dangling from the helicopter. When all are secured, it's up, up, and away . . . for a very breezy ride.

Once the scouts determine the beach to be suitable for a visit, the rest of the squad comes ashore, but they are hardly complacent about it. This is a vulnerable moment for the SEALs, and they are extremely cautious at this phase of insertion.

Strike

The mission against the Panamanian patrol boat was a classic strike or direct action mission, a carefully planned, precision attack against a point target under difficult circumstances. Using any special ops unit for such an attack is a lot more expensive, in every respect, than using conventional resources to do the same kind of thing, so there is usually a good reason for sending SEALs to blow the propellers off a boat instead of (for example)

93

Airborne insertions are also typically done at night,
but that makes for dull photographs.

94

One way to make a quick getaway is to call the helo back for a pickup. The crew will toss a ladder over the ramp, and then it's up to the swimmer to climb back aboard.

having an F/A-18 drop a bomb or smart missile on the target. Collateral damage and loss of life has been one of the driving concerns lately; in Panama, certainly, and in Grenada, too, this caution has created risks of its own.

But ambushes and attacks on point targets are still a major talent of SEALs, another area where they compete with the Army's Rangers and Special Forces. These can be conducted in many imaginative ways, most of which are of the high-risk, high-payoff variety (although SEALs sometimes think some of these are high-risk, low-payoff missions).

Ambushes

The ambush is a kind of classic special op mission. SEALs conducted probably thousands of them in Vietnam—and were on the receiving end of quite a few, too. The "plain vanilla" version of the operation works like this: first, find a place where your enemy regularly travels—a road or trail—and find a nice sharp bend in the route. The "kill zone" will be determined by the patrol leader, normally the long axis of what is an L-shaped portion of the road. The leader will position himself at the corner and will control the whole thing, usually with his own fire and with the triggering of a Claymore mine or two.

Ambushes are marvelously effective when everything works properly—the carnage is *incredible*. But if you screw one up, the carnage can be on your end. And ambushes are easy to screw up; the key is fire discipline and timing.

95

The little $50,000 dune buggy called the Desert Patrol Vehicle is a fast, potent machine for rescuing downed pilots, scouting large sections of potential battlefield, or inserting snipers into an operational area. It will do at least 70mph, fly through space, and—with the machine guns and AT-4 rocket launchers—duke it out with carefully selected enemy forces.

SEALs practice executing raids on oil platforms and other semi-urban spaces. These guys have just landed on a ship and, like buccaneers of old, are swarming aboard to take control. US Navy photo by PH2 Milton Savage

The PAS-7 infrared viewing system. SEALs use a variety of sensor systems to inspect terrain at night; thermal imaging systems such as this make objects like people and vehicles instantly visible out of the gloom.

Ambushes don't take a lot of people or a lot of resources (depending on the target, of course), but they do take planning and teamwork.

If available, Claymores are installed along the kill zone with overlapping fields of fire and with careful attention to protecting the team from the substantial back-blast. If the ambush is along a road, detonation cord can be placed in the ditches that survivors will naturally use for cover after the Claymores fire, and they can be taken out with another squeeze on another "clacker," firing the electric blasting cap that will fire the det cord.

When all the preparations are made, the responsibilities and fields of fire assigned, you and the rest of the crew slither into the woodwork without a trace and wait . . . and wait . . . and wait some more. At last, in the distance, somebody is moving toward you; it can be chil-

dren on their way to school, innocent civilians going to market. You have to sit, silently, waiting for them to pass. What if one of the kids sees the Claymore? What if somebody notices your face peeping out of the brush? Anything that can go wrong, will go wrong to somebody, sooner or later—usually sooner—so it pays to set these things up with exquisite attention to detail.

The way these things are *supposed* to work, an enemy unit will come rolling down the road. With luck (for you, anyway) they will fit the ambush resources; don't pop a Claymore against a platoon of main battle tanks, for example. But if any enemy squad comes bopping down the bunny trail (laughing, playing radios the way they sometimes do), everybody in the ambush waits for the signal to fire. That signal is usually the patrol leader's detonation of the Claymores, hurling their pellets in wide, deadly arcs. If the timing is right and the patrol is within the kill zone, they will all go down—maybe. Some guys are just luckier than others, and fit into a hole in the pattern of the spray of ball bearings. Others may be outside the kill zone. Regardless, this is the time to use all those marksmanship skills they taught you at BUD/S and since. You engage the closest guy with a gun in your field of fire (got a round in the chamber? safety off?), and you keep engaging until there is no more resistance or the patrol leader calls, "Cease fire!" There will be a terrible mess where the patrol was, and this will be a good time to start moving toward the exits.

Ambushes go wrong in lots of ways. Often, the enemy doesn't cooperate. They either won't show up, or they send the wrong victims (like tanks), or they decide not to use the road today, but move along in the woods—where you're hiding. Or they notice you before they get to the kill zone, and then it's *turnabout is fair play*. Then it's your turn to be the vic-

Conflict resolution and power projection in the special operations community generally means something like this—either threatening or actually using deadly force against people to make them behave.

There is something extremely primitive about much of the work of a SEAL team; while drivers of stealth bombers and F-15 Strike Eagles operate multimillion dollar weapons systems in relative comfort, SEALs use skills as old as war. This swim pair crawls up out of the surf, just as their forefathers did in World War II, for a peek inland, hoping and praying that there won't be an enemy sentry on top of the sand dune.

USAF helos support US Navy SEALs in the new cooperative relationship called "joint operations." This kind of integration has had profound effects on things like radios, weapons, training, and doctrine, ensuring that different services can all "play off the same sheet of music," as the operators like to say.

tim—and practice those escape-and-evasion skills they taught you in BUD/S. Just remember what they told you at BUD/S: The only easy day was yesterday.

Raids

The diversion operation at Mina Sa'Ud that helped kick off Desert Storm was one kind of raid, as was the attack on the Noriega

Neville Jet, the rescue of Sir Paul Scoon, and hundreds of similar missions executed by SEALs since World War II. Raids are quick-in, quick-out strikes against high-value targets that can't be attacked efficiently or effectively otherwise. This is another area where SEALs compete with the Army, whose Rangers are masters of the art of the raid. Rangers, however, are specialists in the "blunt instrument"

This role-playing sentry might have a bit of a prob-lem—and a headache not even Anacin could help. Much of the training, equipment, and doctrine used by SEALs today is oriented toward dealing with un-conventional forces like terrorists.

style of raid, with lots of people (very large, muscular ones) and lots of firepower landing on top of an enemy target, typically by parachute, and ripping it to shreds.

The SEAL raid is more surgical and subtle. It still might arrive by parachute, but—unlike with our beloved Ranger Regiment—the enemy target of a SEAL op might never know what hit them. That's because a SEAL strike mission might only involve two men, a sniper and his spotter/security man. With their big .50-caliber sniper rifle and woodcraft skills, these two can move across terrain unseen and disappear into the woodwork.

(Rangers attempting this would leave a trail of scorched earth and destruction visible at a mile). Then the sniper team can sit and wait until the SCUDs come home—and then drill holes in their rocket motors from a mile and a half, without anybody knowing where the bullets came from or how it happened. That same sniper team can, if desired, kill a senior enemy staff officer or commander riding in his Mercedes, pick off a tank commander standing in his hatch, or disable an aircraft taxiing for take-off. In fact, people who weren't part of the Neville Jet take-down op during Operation Just Cause wonder why forty SEALs were

An electrical blasting cap, fresh from the box, ready to prime any military explosive. It contains three stages of material, each setting off the next. The last, *a material called PETN, will reliably set off just about anything.*

sent across the airfield to attack the jet when a sniper team ought to have been able to do it from the safety of the far side of the runways.

Among the most challenging kind of raid SEALs train for is the counterterrorist hostage rescue mission. This is the kind of op that you only get one shot at; it has to be done perfectly or the wrong folks get killed. Consequently SEALs practice all the ancient arts of rapid insertion, extraction, close-quarters target identification, and precision shooting. According to people who've been there, you've got seven seconds in a room with the bad guys to conduct business—sort out the good from the bad, kill the bad guys, protect the good guys—or the operation goes to hell. When you consider that this must often be done at night, in unfamiliar territory, with alert and fanatic enemies, this becomes a tall order. But it can be done, and has, successfully.

Killing People and Destroying Things

A sad but unavoidable consequence of all military missions involves taking perfectly good buildings, airplanes, vehicles, bridges, boats, and people, then taking them apart and converting them into smaller, less useful junk. This process is generally thought to help ac-

A mixed bag of things that go bump in the night— TNT, dynamite, and det cord, with a partial box of blasting caps (time fuse variety). These explosives are quite stable and difficult to detonate without a blasting cap. For example, to prime the dynamite you have to poke a hole in it with a pointed tool, then insert the blasting cap-fuse assembly.

Kids—don't try this at home! Somebody's used a lot of explosive to do a bit of body and fender work on this old car.

complish national policy objectives. While this behavior isn't always considered very nice, it usually works. This is conflict resolution, US Navy SEALs style.

There are many ways SEALs use to accomplish their mission, but basically there are only two fundamental techniques used by the teams. One of these uses individual weapons—rifles, machine guns, mortars—to engage other hostile forces. The other involves using explosives in one form or another to blow things up. "Hostile forces" is a military expression for the loyal soldiers or sailors opposing the SEAL mission, and "engage" is a military expression for the business of shooting up these folks in an organized way. If this seems like kindergarten, it is only because we generally talk around the seamier side of the business of war.

SEAL missions often involve the destruction of some enemy facility—a radio transmitter, a bridge, a bunker complex, a headquarters, or (as in the attack on the *Presidente Porras* in the beginning of this book) a naval vessel. This usually involves the use of high explosives in one of many forms, and one thing most SEALs quickly discover in BUD/S is that

explosives are *fun.* As one blaster says with a smirk, "There are very few of life's troubles that can't be cured with high explosives."

A Short Course in Demolitions and High Explosives

Despite what you hear, high explosives are quite safe to handle and are actually difficult to detonate. Most of the military varieties can be pounded with a hammer (old, runny dynamite excepted) without going off. One of the best materials for blasting passages through coral reefs is a simple mixture of fertilizer and diesel fuel. You can break off a chunk of TNT from a quarter-pound block and set fire to it; so it's not only a great explosive, it's also a great heat source for warming up your lunch. C4, the famous "plastic explosive," looks, feels, and acts like putty—a white material that you can easily form and shape with your fingers, in complete safety. The same is true of virtually all other military explosives, with the possible exception of dynamite, a combination of nitroglycerine and gun-cotton, that can become quite unstable if stored improperly. Most of these materials can sit on the shelf for decades without any significant decay, and it isn't unusual to be issued cratering charges, for example, that were made during World War II.

For these and other reasons, explosives are very interesting and useful materials, available in many forms. There is Primacord or "det cord," a material that looks like fuse, a flexible plastic-like quarter-inch cord that contains a very high explosive, PETN, and is used to connect main charges. The PETN cord is set off with a blasting cap or other charge—then it explodes at a linear rate of about four miles per second with enough force to detonate any US military explosive the cord is tied to. It is very handy stuff for making a lot of little charges all go off at the same time—and other, sneakier applications discussed later.

In every case, including that of dynamite, you must work hard and carefully to actually get the stuff to go off. And that's accomplished with a little device that is quite dangerous and that will go off if you fail to handle it with care, caution, and respect—the blasting cap. These come in two flavors: electric and fused. Both are tubes of aluminum or copper, a quarter of an inch in diameter, partially filled with a three-stage mixture of specialized explosives, an ignition charge, a priming charge, and a base charge. Although things happen quickly, these charges go off in sequence, and the last one, the base charge, is the one that *should* set off the main charge.

As an example, let's set off a one-pound block of TNT. The main charge comes in a cardboard tube with a threaded receptacle on the ends to hold the blasting cap. We'll use common fuse instead of an electrical cap for this charge; it's more traditional. Also less safe.

First we take the fuse, cut six inches off the end and discard it. This should remove any contaminated and unreliable material. Then we cut a section six feet long, light one end, and time the delay. After about four minutes, a little flash of fire will come from the end. Note the time, divide by six, and you know what the delay of the fuse is in seconds per foot; normally it is about forty seconds per foot. Now, using your combination tool designed for demolitions work, cut a good, healthy length of fuse sufficient for five minutes' delay. The ends should be clean, square cuts.

Remove a blasting cap from the storage box where they are kept for safety and inspect the fuse well for foreign matter. *Gently* slip the fuse into the open end—about an inch—and into contact with the ignition charge. Crimp the fuse to the cap with the crimper part of the tool, about a quarter inch from the end of the cap. Now gently insert the cap into the priming well of the TNT block, place it on the ground, and extend the fuse so that it doesn't coil over on itself. We could use a fuse-lighter to get things started, but you might as well learn the traditional way first: split the fuse end about half an inch, insert a match head in the core, and strike it. The match will ignite the black powder inside, a bit of flame will sputter, a little smoke will be emitted,

Emplacing an M18 Claymore. The device is not much more than a slab of C4 explosives and a lot of ball bearings, electrically primed. It sprays a cloud of steel pellets that will kill or maim anyone within about fifty meters to the front.

and it is time to vacate the premises. It is considered good manners to shout, "Fire in the hole!" at this point unless there are bad guys in the vicinity. You walk, not run, well away, take cover, note the time, and await developments.

When the fuse burns down inside a non-electric blasting cap, a little squirt of flame shoots out, into the cap. If everything works as planned, the ignition charge goes off, then the priming charge, which detonates the base charge of the cap, and that little blast will usually set off the TNT. There will be a loud *Boom!*, and dust and rocks will scatter for a hundred meters in all directions. But don't expect any gaping crater—even a pound of TNT won't do much unless it is artfully placed and prepared. Instead, we have a patch of ground that is lightly depressed and not much more.

Explosives are used to do very specific things and are used with mathematical precision. You can cut a twelve-inch diameter tree with a half-pound block and have it fall across

The M67 hand grenade is thrown like a baseball. With practice you can put it into a machine-gun pit, a bunker, or a room. Without practice it tends to bounce back, fall short, or otherwise embarrass its thrower.

a roadway, blocking traffic. You can make a ribbon out of C4 plastic explosive, stick it to a steel girder, and cut a bridge support. You can shape it into a flat diamond and wrap it around an eighteen-inch diameter ship's propeller shaft, prime both points with blasting caps, and cut off the shaft neatly when the charge goes off. Put two identical charges on both sides of a concrete wall or abutment and prime electrically so both go off at the same instant, and a small amount of explosive (a pound and a half per foot of thickness) will crumble the concrete.

The most common application of explosives for SEALs has been clearing beach obstacles prior to amphibious landings, a technique developed to a minor art form by the UDT swimmers during World War II and Korea. Besides that use, vast quantities of C4

went up in smoke in Vietnam and, more recently, in the Gulf, blowing up bunkers and creating diversions. You can make a foxhole in a hurry with it, crater a road, cut a railroad line or a thick telephone cable. In the form of a Bangalore torpedo (a long section of steel pipe filled with explosive) you can blast a gap through a barbed wire obstacle or a minefield. It is mighty handy stuff.

Det cord, all by itself, has an interesting application for those occasional ambushes where you have plenty of time to set up shop. It can be electrically primed and hidden in roadside ditches alongside the "kill zone." When the ambush is initiated, you can be reasonably certain that the survivors of the first blast of small arms fire will dive for the presumed protection of the handy ditch. If the SEAL with the "hell box" (as the blasting ma-

106

chine is called) remembers to twist the handle about now, the det cord will explode in the ditch, adding to the consternation and woe of the enemy force.

Claymore Mines

The Claymore mine was developed in Vietnam to deal with those nasty situations when a couple of hundred little fellers in black paja-mas were swarming across the barbed wire defenses of a compound with intentions of committing mayhem on the residents. The Claymore is a simple little package of C4 explosive and a few hundred steel ball bearings, fired with an electric blasting cap and a "clacker" (a one-handed electric generator that, when squeezed, will fire the cap). When the explosive detonates, the ball bearings

If this sniper team wasn't posing for the camera you wouldn't know they were there at all. The rifle is a bolt-action .50-caliber model designed specifically for special operations use. The bolt has to be removed to load each round. Its effective range is about two kilometers—more than a mile and a half.

Haskins .50-caliber sniper rifle. Despite the rumor, there is no prohibition against using the .50-caliber against individual enemy targets. This weapon is designed, among other things, to kill a man with the first shot at ranges over a half mile. The tremendous recoil is partly absorbed by twin hydraulic shock absorbers in the stock—and partially by the shoulder of the firer.

107

A sniper team in "ghillie" suits. These camouflage suits are handmade by the men as part of their training at the Special Operations Target Interdic- *tion Course. In them they blend into the terrain, virtually disappearing—although they do have a tendency to stand out a bit on the street.*

spray a wide area with deadly effect, usually helping to convince the enemy force that there may be other, better, things to do than to attack this particular place.

Claymores have since become favorites for temporary defensive fighting positions and for ambushes, where they excel. Like virtually all other weapons, they are not perfect or foolproof. One sneaky trick the VC learned was to find them and turn them around.

The guy with the "clacker" in an ambush setup has to be a very cool dude, sufficiently self-disciplined to wait until the enemy is properly within the kill zone before firing the weapon. Lots of perfectly good ambushes have been ruined by the premature detonation of the Claymore, removing the element of surprise quickly and completely.

SEALs carry a Claymore or two along on some of their excursions, the whole kit of mine, clacker, wire, and blasting cap all stored neatly in a little bundle complete with carrying strap.

.50-Caliber Sniper Rifle

One fine, somewhat neglected military art is that of the sniper. SEALs and Green Berets study this skill at the Target Interdiction Course, part of the Special Operations Command Center and School at the Army's Fort Bragg, North Carolina. Here, out among the weeds and chiggers, apprentice SEAL snipers learn how to move invisibly across any terrain, to build a hide so natural that an enemy can stand on top of it and not know that two Navy SEALs are in residence below, and to shoot so well that enemy soldiers over a half mile away die with the first shot, tank commanders standing in the turrets of their tanks lose their heads (literally), and antennas and vision ports on armored vehicles become useless.

The key to all this is a relatively simple, relatively ancient weapon—the rifle. The one favored by special operators like the SEALs these days is the big .50-caliber single-shot, bolt-action model that weighs about twenty pounds with scope and bipod. For a variety of reasons the big half-inch bullet will fly very accurately, very far. It will reliably strike a man-sized target so far away that the noise from its firing is practically inaudible, out to ranges of two kilometers, more than a mile and a half. But to achieve such accuracy requires far more than just an accurate weapon and sights. A SEAL sniper team out in the bush must deal with wind, moving targets, slant angles, and heat distortion.

Snipers work as two-man teams: the shooter and the spotter. They are inserted near their objective by boat or parachute, or swim ashore from a submarine, or come by Volkswagen bus—whatever works for the tactical situation. They will travel the last kilometer or so to their hide by crawling. It can take a day or more. Their weapons and equipment are contained in a "drag bag," pulled along behind each. Under cover of darkness, they carefully, methodically carve a hole in the ground, then re-cover it so artfully that it seems perfectly undisturbed. In this hole the pair will live for a day or two, observing, recording, and possibly reporting by radio. Normally the sniper's mission will not include actually firing on an enemy force but calling in artillery or aviation to do the job.

Determining range to the target and wind effect are the two principal problems confronting the sniper team, and the pair will expend considerable effort preparing to fire the first shot. A big .50-caliber round is inserted into the breech, the bolt brought forward, locked, and the sights carefully aligned on a computed aim point.

The spotter uses a compact telescope to look downrange. Instead of watching the target, the spotter watches for the *bullet* as it streaks toward the victim. With proper training and the right weather conditions, you can actually see a bullet and the vapor trail produced as it flies through the atmosphere. The spotter reports the point of impact to the shooter for any corrections.

Another version of the .50-caliber sniper rifle, used in Desert Storm.

Chapter 6

Special Boat Squadrons— The Brown Water Navy

As mentioned earlier, the Special Boat Squadrons have typically been somewhat neglected in favor of the higher profile SEAL teams in the development of Naval Special Warfare. That's too bad because the boats have as rich a combat history as the teams, and both have worked closely together for nearly three decades. In fact, one of the big selling points for Naval Special Warfare in the competitive business of special operations is the unique resource SPECWARCOM has in its fleet of boats designed to take the fight close to the beach and up all those lazy rivers.

The Special Boat Squadrons are teamed with the SEALs to provide a kind of mutual support. And, just as the SEALs have a variety of weapons to choose from for their missions, the SBS crews have a menu of boats as well. There are little IBS inflatables, RIBs, PBRs, and fast-attack patrol boats. Most are stunningly fast, with thirty-knot-plus speeds . . . although you only get speeds like that from an IBS (a little seven-man rubber duck) when all the BUD/S are screaming and the students are paddling like crazy.

Mission mobility for Naval Special Warfare provides an extremely diverse set of problems for the "Coronado Yacht Club." Here is a breakdown of the three basic areas of respon-

Thirty-foot rigid hull inflatable boat (RIB) with fire team of SEALs embarked. The crew are from the Special Boat Squadrons.

sibility for the SBS part of NSW. But don't think that there's a sharp line between any of these assignments—the real world has a way of mixing and matching them. The boat that is primarily intended for coastal patrol may find itself occasionally on a riverine mission, or executing some exotic special operations support assignment.

Coastal Patrol and Interdiction

The first of these, requiring the biggest vessels, is the coastal patrol mission. The offshore patrol and interdiction mission is very different than, say, the clandestine insertion of a couple of combat swimmers for a demolition raid. It takes a good-sized vessel to provide the kind of platform needed to stay offshore for very long, to provide reasonable comfort for the crew, and to have the speed and firepower to accomplish anything useful. These missions are currently assigned to the Patrol Boat Coastal (PBC), Mk III Swift Patrol Boat, and the Mk IV Patrol Boat.

Neither the PBR or PBL provide much speed or comfort out past the surf zone; they're flat water boats with a specific set of missions. For the offshore jobs, where the Sea State goes up to five or so and the waves swell up to twelve feet, even froggy SEALs want something sturdy and stable. That pretty well eliminates the light little flat-bottomed boats in favor of something longer and beamier,

The Naval Special Warfare community finally gets a real ship in the form of the new Patrol Boat, Coastal (PBC) vessel. While it isn't all that fast, light, or stealthy, it at least provides organic support for long missions offshore, with facilities for SEALs or other small teams of operators.

The Mk III patrol boat was intended to be a fast, in-shore weapons platform that can mount mortars, heavy machine guns, and a big 40mm canon. With a length of 65 feet and three high-power, light-weight diesel engines and an extensive rack of radars and radios, the Mk III is a fast, potent little vessel. Its missions include coastal and river patrol, gunfire support, and insertion and extraction of a complete SEAL squad.

with a nice, sharp V-hull to slide through the waves instead of pound along on top of them.

Patrol Boat, Coastal (PBC)

The PBC is something of a major change for the Naval Special Warfare community—the introduction of an entirely new class of ship to support NAVSPECWARCOM missions. In the past such support has been improvised, based on whatever happens to be around. The PC-1 class formalizes the support.

Ships of this class, starting with the *Cyclone* (PC-1), are designed for serious patrol work, their primary mission. Naval Special Warfare support is secondary, but a dedicated assignment. With an overall length of 170 feet, the PBCs are big enough for serious offshore work, reasonably comfortable, and commodi-ous enough for a rather large number of embarked SEALs and Naval Special Warfare players.

The ships are the biggest platform the Special Boat Squadrons have ever had. They're funded by Special Operations Command and are assigned to the NSW Groups at Coronado and Little River, but are likely to be forward based. There will be a total of thirteen of the PBCs when the program is complete.

Obviously, it is hard to be very covert with 170 feet of warship. Rather than sneaking and peeking like the little boats, the PCs will be used to "show the flag" while maintaining a US presence in regions where the National Command Authority wants a show of force. The ships will be tasked with monitoring and detection missions, escort operations, noncom-

The RIB is quite capable of getting airborne, and throwing its passengers overboard, too, if they aren't careful.

The coxswain's control console is pretty fancy for a rubber boat, but appropriate for such an expensive, high-performance craft.

batant evacuation, and foreign internal defense—all pretty much the plain-vanilla patrol mission assigned to any of the Navy's or Coast Guard's smaller ships.

The more interesting missions, and the ones the Naval Special Warfare community is involved in, are for long-range insertion and extraction of SEAL teams, tactical-swimmer operations, intelligence collection, operational deception, and coastal or riverine support.

The PBC's steel hull with aluminum superstructure has a beam of twenty-five feet and a draft of about eight feet; it displaces about 330 tons (full load). Propulsion comes from twin diesels that can drive the ship at thirty-five knots. A tank of fuel (about 13,000 gallons) will give a range of about 2,000 nautical miles at a moderate cruise speed of twelve knots. The ship will tolerate Sea State 5 condi-

tions—rough seas with waves of 8–12 feet. There is a platform on the stern for launching and recovering combat swimmers, and the ships each have two CRRCs available for SEAL operations.

Normal complement is four officers and twenty-four enlisted personnel. Unlike previous SBS vessels, the commander of the PBC ships is not likely to be a SEAL but a surface warfare officer. While there is some apprehension about this, there is also the realization that this is an entirely new asset for the community, with a somewhat different mission—and how it all works out remains to be seen. There will probably be at least a few SEALs assigned. Besides the crew, there is berthing for a nine-man SOF or law-enforcement detachment aboard.

Appropriate to its size and missions, the

114

PCs will be the most heavily armed of Naval Special Warfare craft. A Mk 38 25mm rapid-fire gun is installed, along with a station for the Stinger antiaircraft missile system. Four mounts for heavy automatic weapons are available for the Mk 19 40mm grenade launcher, M2 .50-caliber machine gun, and the M60 7.62mm machine gun. For antiship missile defense, a Mk 52 chaff/decoy system is installed.

Mk III Swift Patrol Boat

The Mk III is a big, 65-foot boat designed back in the 1960s with a coastal mission in mind. These boats have been used extensively in combat over the years, particularly to patrol the waters off the coast of Vietnam and, more recently, the Latin American coastal waters used by drug traffickers and the Persian Gulf waters in support of Desert Storm. The basic mission is to serve as a high-speed weapons platform for Naval Special Warfare units. The deck is reinforced to tolerate recoil stresses from the many weapons that can be mounted on the Mk III—any mix of 20mm cannon, 81mm or 60mm mortar, Mk 19 40mm grenade launcher, .50-caliber machine gun, and the faithful old M60 7.62mm machine gun.

The boat is rated at thirty-plus knots, needs a crew of eleven, and can stay out up to five days. It is powered by three big diesel engines installed in an all-aluminum hull with a low-profile radar and acoustic signature (for this kind of boat, anyway) that makes it comparatively easy to accomplish some kinds of covert missions. The Navy will tell you officially that it is "reasonably" stable in "moderately" heavy seas, but most experienced offshore operators will tell you that a 65-foot hull fits neatly in the troughs of most any sea and will wallow like a pig in mud given half an opportunity.

But Naval Special Warfare boats aren't intended to be pleasure craft. The Mk III is tasked with patrol and interdiction missions, with fire-support missions against targets ashore or afloat, and the insertion of SEAL team elements. One of their users, an SBS unit commander, says of them, "They've lasted

SEALs support a US Marine Corps beach landing operation during Operation Desert Storm. US Navy photo

through everything we've sent them to, from Vietnam to the Persian Gulf—and in fact the Persian Gulf is where they've gotten their heaviest workout." The Mk III is an old boat now, nearing retirement. An improved model, the Mk IV, is in service, but a completely new version, to be called the Mk V, is in the long design and acquisition process.

Mk IV Patrol Boat

The Sea Spectre 68-foot patrol boat is an improved version of the Mk III, an evolution of a proven design with some substantial upgrades. The missions, specifications, and weapons remain about the same, but the boat is designed to be more easily adaptable to the wide variety of missions that such boats are tasked for. Like its older brother, it is not a heavy weather offshore boat (that doesn't mean you don't have to operate in those conditions, just that you'll be uncomfortable when you do).

Special Operations Support Mission

Support for special operations doesn't have the same kind of requirements for station time that patrol does, and the boats used for inserting and supporting SEALs and other

A Swimmer Delivery Vehicle (SDV) being deployed from a Dry Deck Shelter (DDS) of a submarine. US Navy photo

Locking out of a sub. Rigging the SDV is the business of the members of the SDV support unit, who are tasked with maintaining a complicated system plus maintaining their SEAL skills. US Navy photo

SOC operators are designed with things other than comfort in mind: speed, range, capacity, and a low radar signature are far more important than stability or fuel economy.

And the SBS crews and boats aren't always supporting strictly SEALs or Naval Special Warfare personnel; part of the idea of the Joint Special Operations Forces when it was established was to coordinate and integrate all the operators going downrange. So these SBS and NSW assets give rides to Green Berets and Rangers as well as to SEALs, and even to the occasional Force Recon Marine.

Rigid Inflatable Boats (RIB)

RIBs are the boat of the hour. Everybody's making and using them. Pretty soon you'll probably be able to take a Caribbean cruise on one. They're simple, cheap, fairly economical, and faster than a speeding bullet. They are used by the Navy, the Coast Guard, and many foreign nations. They combine some of the best features of rigid hull and inflatable designs in one fast, stable, buoyant platform.

There are three variants of the big rubber duck used by the SEALs: 24-foot, 30-foot, and 10-meter RIBs. All use fiberglass hulls with a V-shaped cross section, offering stability, a rigid motor mount, and firm footing, along with an inflatable gunwale section. The inflatable part of the boat is fabricated from an extremely tough material, a combination of hypalon neoprene and nylon reinforced fabric. It won't shed bullets, but it will take a lot of lesser abuse, including the pounding you get from jamming around offshore, punching through the waves. The hammering a boat takes in normal service can be pretty severe, cracking fiberglass and aluminum hulls with the constant flexing. That is not a problem with an inflatable.

The RIBs are extremely tolerant, for a small boat, of heavy seas. With light loads the boats have operated offshore in extreme conditions—Sea State 6 and winds of forty-five knots. That means waves up to twenty feet high, when even SEALs would rather be ashore, even at BUD/S. While the boats can operate in such conditions, they normally don't go out when things get that bad; the SOP calls for a Sea State 5/thirty-four-knot wind limit on use. All the boats are normally crewed by three SBS sailors.

The 24-foot RIB weighs in at about 10,000 pounds fully loaded. It is powered by a single Volvo inboard engine/outboard drive powerplant and has a rated maximum speed of twenty-eight knots. Range is 175 nautical miles at twenty-five-knot speeds. Even this little boat mounts a radar—and an M60 7.62mm machine gun. Its principal mission is to deliver a single SEAL fire team (half a squad, four men) to an insertion point. It isn't the stealthiest way to insert a SEAL element on a covert mission, but not all missions require invisibility.

The 30-foot RIB is quite similar to the 24-foot version, but with two engines driving water jet drives and a higher rated maximum speed of thirty-two knots. The 30-footer is, as a result, half again heavier, weighing in at a combat weight of about 15,000 pounds. Range is slightly less, at 150 nautical miles, and the payload is a bit bigger.

The biggest of the breed is the 10-meter (33-foot) inflatable. This one will accommodate a whole squad. This means that an entire eight-man SEAL combat element can be cold, wet, and miserable while they huddle behind the dubious armor of two thin sheets of high-tech rubber and about two feet of compressed air on the run in to that hostile shore. The boat can be pumped up to forty knots, just in case the coxswain decides to race an aircraft carrier or perhaps outflank the fleet. And when he gets in range, this inflatable warship carries two weapons mounts accommodating

either M60s or Mk 19 grenade launchers. There's enough fuel aboard for about an eight-hour mission, providing a range of around 250 nautical miles.

Combat Rubber Raiding Craft (CRRC)

One of the most used and useful boats in the inventory is a kind of war-surplus model left over from World War II, the CRRC—the legendary little rubber duck. Originally designed as a life raft, the boat has been adopted and adapted to all sorts of offensive missions. Marines use it, the Army Rangers and Green Berets use it, and of course the SEALs use it, for clandestine surface insertions and extractions. The CRRC weighs only 265 pounds. It gets tossed out of C-130 airplanes or from cargo helicopters, along with the SEALs, into the ocean. It is also launched from submarines, either from the surface or submerged, or gets chucked over the side of larger surface craft.

It's only about fifteen feet long, with a six-foot beam, but it will do about twenty knots. That, of course, requires an outboard engine, a single fifty-five horsepower powerplant with an eighteen-gallon fuel bladder providing a range of about sixty-five miles. That offers

The DDS is a temporary, hangar-like arrangement that bolts to the hull of the sub. It can accommodate a whole SEAL squad in relative comfort, or the squad and the SDV, in which case the squad is less comfortable. US Navy photo

over-the-horizon capability, but—trust me on this—you don't want to ride one in to the beach from over the horizon except on the *nicest* of days.

It is an extremely versatile piece of gear. While civilians spend hundreds or thousands of dollars on health clubs and Nordic Track exercise machines, the Navy uses the CRRC at BUD/S to build better bodies eight ways. In fact, the BUD/S instructors have discovered that you don't need fancy machines or chrome-plated weights, just a CRRC; if you have the students hold one overhead for a few minutes it *really* works those upper-body muscles. And, for a little extra help for those who need it, the CRRC can easily hold plenty of wet sand, bringing its weight up to something more challenging.

These inflatables have another virtue lacking in most other Navy property: they are, at times, considered disposable. Rather than go through the time and trouble to bring one back aboard a submerged sub, you may, during real world combat operations, stick your dive knife into one when you're done with your mission and let it sink to the bottom, engine and all. Just make sure that the submarine is standing by for you first!

SEALs are hauled back aboard a Patrol Boat, River (PBR)

Swimmer Delivery Vehicle (SDV) Mk VIII

Perhaps the most interesting, least publicized, most covert boat the Naval Special Warfare community operates is the wet submersible called the SDV Mk VIII. It's an odd little submarine SEALs use for fast, covert sub-surface insertions. The SDV is like a little speed boat, with rechargeable batteries and an electric motor for propulsion. Like other submarines, the SDV is visually blind and relies on sensors and instrumentation to navigate without bumping into things.

The embarked SEALs climb into a fully enclosed cabin. Although they wear scuba or closed-circuit breathing systems for backup and for work outside the vehicle, the SDV has its own supply of breathing air.

SDVs are launched from surface craft sometimes, but the dry deck shelter (DDS) attached to a submarine is a more typical point of departure. The DDS is like a small hanger, big enough for the SDV and with enough room for the swimmers to enter from the sub and climb into the SDV. The DDS is gradually flooded, the hatch opened, and out goes the SDV in search of adventure. The divers are now essentially in an expensive tin can full of water. It can be a cold ride. As one of its users says:

"It's a strange ride. You can't see out. You fly on instruments the entire time. You are a diver the entire time you're in it. The SDV provides more speed and range than swimming. Quite honestly, the boat will go farther than the man will. Exposure to the cold and to the ambient sea pressure put tremendous strains on the human body that become a limiting factor for missions with the SDV. I don't think it's used enough, perhaps because its reliability hasn't always been too great. It is a complicated thing to support and deliver. But if you plan its use properly, if you get it within its range, it is an extremely effective tool because it is almost nondetectable. The ability to deliver either SEALs or ordnance is just phenomenal!"

The vehicle has its own support unit, the SDV team, within SPECWARCOM. These teams maintain and operate the SDV, SEALs who actually man the boats on missions. An operator and a navigator are always assigned; both are fully qualified SEALs who have what amounts to a kind of bus driver job in addition to the usual combat assignments in the objective area.

The SDV is rated to carry six swimmers and their equipment, including the crew of two. A sonar sensor (for object avoidance) and an inertial navigation system allow the operator to cruise around underwater. A third sensor system is sometimes installed as part of a developmental program, but that remains "buggy," a side-scanning sonar for target identification of objects like mines as well as to record bottom contour. Not too surprisingly, a lot of specific performance information about these exotic little boats is classified. While the specifics are secret, we are authorized to hint a lot: The vehicle is about twice as fast as a submerged swimmer; vehicle endurance is probably a lot longer than crew endurance; and the SDV will tolerate up to 500 feet of water pressure without failing, and that's a lot farther than the crew will go before their subsystems start to fail! We could tell you more, but then we'd have to kill you.

Actually, though, the whole vehicle was extremely classified for a very long time. It couldn't be moved without being covered, and of course no photographs could be released showing it. But a few years ago, the then commander of SPECWARCOM decided the SDV would be a nice addition to the unit's annual float in the Coronado 4th of July parade and ordered it displayed on the flatbed trailer, along with the usual "cammied" Naval SPECWARCOM warriors. That's the way it is sometimes around Naval Special Warfare—things that are super-secret on one day and in one place are proudly displayed to the world the next.

Riverine Patrol and Interdiction

SEAL experience in Vietnam strongly demonstrated the need for good shallow-draft boats with plenty of speed, stealth, space for

Boat coxswain. Although the SBS coxswains don't go through BUD/S and aren't SEALs, they play an essential role in Naval Special Warfare.

combat-equipped SEALs, and provisions for both defending and attacking when in contact with enemy forces. That mission still exists today, in Latin America, where the US is involved in a quiet war in the backwaters of the Amazon basin and elsewhere. The boats from that previous war, along with some new ones, are helping to fight this one. Sometimes SEALs are embarked, sometimes not. In some cases the operators are foreign military or law enforcement people who are equipped and trained by the US, often by SEALs in the Foreign Internal Defense mission.

Patrol Boat, River (PBR)

The PBR has been around since quite

The SBS crews are the unsung heroes of Naval Special Warfare—or so they say, anyway. But at least they aren't shy when the media shows up.

early in the Vietnam war. It is still serving long after most of its crews have retired, a design with an interesting history.

When SEAL Team One packed its bags and shipped out to the combat zone in 1966 it was pretty much without a really good boat to support its new missions. Existing Navy LCPL (Landing Craft, Personnel, Launch) fleet craft had been modified for the purpose but just didn't seem suitable for the riverine mission of fast, long-range, shallow-draft patrol. That's why, in September 1965, the Navy's Bureau of Ships published a request for bids on a twenty-five to thirty-knot boat with a "dead-in-the-water" draft of eighteen inches and a draft at speed of only nine inches. A slightly modified commercial design from the Hattaras Yacht Company was selected, a 28-foot boat with "Jacuzzi" type propulsion.

The prototype was delivered only two weeks later. After testing, the design was modified, lengthened a bit to thirty-one feet,

and christened the PBR Mk I. The boats were being delivered to the Navy only a year after the program began. Not much later they were zooming around the Mekong Delta, trading shots with the VC and providing a kind of taxi service for SEALs off on nocturnal excursions.

The PBR was designed for high-speed patrol and insertion operations in rivers and bays. It is a heavily armed and armored boat, designed for combat at close quarters, with special ceramic armor similar to that used on tanks applied to the vessels' crew compartment. The hull is made of thick, reinforced fiberglass and is designed to accept the stresses of recoiling heavy machine guns and grenade launchers. The current PBR in service is 32-feet long, with a beam of about 12-feet. It weighs about 18,000 pounds—light enough to be transported on C-5 Galaxy aircraft.

While fairly ancient as military systems go, it is still an amazing boat. The two big

This High-Speed Boat (HSB) has just shot up a golf course with that big .50-caliber machine gun, terrorizing much of the tourist trade of Coronado, California, without so much as an apology. The HSB was originally intended to catch the small and medium-sized vessels that had been tormenting merchant and military shipping in odd corners of the world during the last decade or two. Very few of the costly, complex boats were purchased, and they've mainly been used as "adversaries" to train the Navy to deal with the fast, hit-and-run attacks of the sort mounted by Iraq and Iran. Even so, the HSBs were used during the deception campaign against Iraqi forces near Kuwait City, zooming along just off the beach, firing machine guns and tossing explosive charges over the side.

One of the 24-foot RIBs at speed. These extremely popular boats are used for many purposes by SEALs and other hard-charging units. They tolerate a lot of abuse (not including bullets), are fast, stable, and relatively easy to maintain and transport.

The Patrol Boat, Light (PBL) is a Boston Whaler with an attitude problem. The attitude comes from all those machine guns and the knowledge that, no matter how many holes the enemy puts in the hull, the fragments of the boat are unsinkable. US Navy photo

General Electric diesel engines will tootle along quietly or crank up 215hp each when required. Those engines each drive a 14-inch Jacuzzi pump; the water squirts out of 5.75-inch nozzles, making the boat go faster than thirty knots—in excess of thirty-five miles an hour to you landlubbers. Of course, that's with the water jets clean, and they do clog up. It has a range of 200 miles on 160 gallons of fuel. Normal crew complement is four.

A lot of bullets have dinged off the hulls and armor of PBRs, and a lot of crewmen have died aboard them. The boats have done a lot of shooting of their own. Standard equipment includes a tub-mounted twin M2 .50-caliber machine gun system in the bow; that's industrial-strength firepower guaranteed to "clean the clock" of almost any point target within two kilometers. There is also a pedestal mount for another M2 .50-caliber and a mount for the marvelous Mk 19 grenade launcher, a type of machine gun that fires 40mm, baseball-sized projectiles to better than two kilometers. As options you can sometimes get a 60mm mortar installed, with or without M60 machine-guns, and additional .50-caliber and 40mm machine

guns mounted amidship. Of the more than 500 PBRs built since 1966 only twenty-four or so remain in service. A new design is in the works.

Patrol Boat, Light (PBL)

The PBL is another modified off-the-shelf civilian design from that distant era; still in use is the 25-foot military version of the Boston Whaler, an unsinkable little boat powered by a pair of big engines and mounting two heavy weapons, the M2 .50-caliber machine gun and/or the Mk 19 grenade launcher. The PBL is a light, fast, air-portable, quiet, somewhat vulnerable boat that has evolved a bit over the years, but continues to support the riverine mission after almost three decades in the inventory.

Like the PBR, it uses water-jet propulsion to achieve better than thirty-knot speeds on flat water. It will turn on a proverbial dime—in fact, the boat will turn a lot faster than the coxswain and crew will probably find comfortable, a 180-degree about-face in less than 30-feet while doing thirty knots. While the G-load of such a maneuver could easily toss most everybody right out of the boat, it is a handy capability for those times you come blasting around a bend and find a horde of bad guys waiting for your arrival.

Two pedestal-mounted "Ma Duce" heavy machine guns are mounted just forward of the coxswain's position. This provides all-aspect firepower for breaking contact when the crew of three thinks it is necessary. There is also a third mount farther forward, and any combination of .50-caliber and 7.62mm machine guns can be installed.

Although the PBL draws about a foot and a half of water when stopped, at speed it will just about operate in a mud puddle, skimming along on the surface of the water rather than through it. The two engines will run at full throttle for eight hours on a tank of fuel, driving the boat across about 160 nautical miles of river or canal at more than twenty-five knots. It uses standard twin engines, with dual steerage, ignition, and controls for back-up redundancy.

It is an extremely mobile little boat, in and out of the water. The PBL can travel on a conventional trailer, be rigged as a sling load for a helicopter, or be loaded aboard a C-130. A lot of PBLs have traveled to Latin American military forces, where they are justifiably popular with the counter-narcotics forces patrolling the Amazon delta and other riverine battlefields.

Mini-Armored Troop Carrier (MATC)

The MATC is a kind of small landing craft similar to the ones Marines have been using to come ashore for decades, only smaller. It has a flat, ramp-type bow that drops forward to eject a whole platoon of sixteen combat-equipped SEALs onto a beach. It is a riverine craft with shallow draft and all the sea-keeping qualities of a cork. Like the PBR and most other riverine craft, the MATC has a water-jet propulsion system that "vacuums" the boat through the water, Jacuzzi fashion. A crew of three operates the boat.

Its hull is thirty-six feet long, made of aluminum, and is designed for high-speed patrol, interdiction, and combat assault missions on the relatively flat waters of bays, rivers, canals, and protected coastal areas. It is serious about all this—there are seven weapons stations for heavy machine guns or grenade launchers and a 60mm mortar can be installed. It comes with a high-resolution radar and a rack of radios for every taste and purpose. The boat weighs about 25,000 pounds, is good for about thirty knots and a range of 230 nautical miles from 430 gallons of fuel.

In the grand SEAL tradition, the boat is fast and sneaky. It has a low six-foot profile that's hard to see or pick up on radar (well, for a slab-sided metal-hulled boat). The engines are extremely quiet. What this all means is that you can pile a bunch of weapons and troops aboard, run up the river to a likely spot, slide into the weeds and woodwork along the bank, and wait, engine at idle. With good "comms" you can talk to surveillance aircraft overhead, other teams ashore and afloat in the area, and wait for your victim to come chugging down the creek. When the perpetrators of the crime arrive on scene, the MATC has the troops and the firepower to negotiate with just about anybody and win through intimidation.

Chapter 7

Leader's Recon

Before a combat operation, particularly ashore, a commander will, time permitting, travel to the objective area for "eyes on" the target, as LT Tom Dietz did before the diversionary raid on the Iraqi coastal defenses in Kuwait. This personal study by a combat commander of an area where conflict will occur is called "leader's recon." There is no good substitute for this kind of personal, direct contact by the combat leader with the battlefield. For people within military communities there are all kinds of battlefields besides the kind we usually think of. Some are institutional, within the unit, while others are the political, doctrinal, policy arenas. For the past fifty years, SEALS have had to adapt to changes in the world, in the US armed forces, in the Navy, and within Naval Special Warfare itself. These internal battles shape the nature of the institution that will fight the wars of the future. These institutional, peacetime conflicts are tremendously dangerous—not for the present, but for the time when push comes to shove, as it always seem to do.

Among the most dangerous things SEALs need to worry about is complacency on their own part, about bad tactical habits, about inexperience and overconfidence. Despite several combat operations over the last couple of decades, the SEAL community today is almost completely inexperienced in war—and this is a dangerous thing. War is different than training, no matter how tough that training may be.

Combat experience is slipping away from the Navy. The last Navy Medal of Honor winner retired in 1992, and nearly all the Vietnam combat veterans have left the formal military service. One of these men with a great deal of combat time is CDR Gary Stubblefield, recently retired but still actively working with Naval Special Warfare as a consultant and contractor. With retirement comes a greater freedom to discuss Naval Special Warfare issues. The following are a kind of "leader's recon" offered by Commander Stubblefield, a selection of opinions and insights about the life and times of SEALs today and in the future. His observations are a rare insight into the challenges of the present and future for Naval Special Warfare.

Deployment & Tasking

"Since the time I started in this business twenty-five years ago, I've seen a lot of changes. One is that now our people expect to receive their missions while sitting here in the States or in some forward-deployed base overseas—receipt of mission from higher authority, rather than developing our own missions from within the area where we will operate. In Vietnam we set up our own bases, designed our own missions, and, unless somebody thought we were doing something really stupid, we were left alone. Now we are directed by higher authority. When Ray Smith was operating in the Gulf, he was getting messages from the CINC saying, 'Conduct SEAL operations here, here, and here.'"

Planning and Accountability

"We've become very good at developing 'overhead' intelligence-collecting from aircraft and satellites. We've lost the ability to develop good 'human intelligence,' the ability to develop information from people, face-to-face. We were *great* at that, and it was so much better than what we even get now from the overhead systems. But you only get human intelligence by living there, by being part of the community, by building rapport with the host nation—it's the only way that will work. Now we do our planning in an insular way.

"Now I receive my intel, develop a concept or a series of options for an operation, and then I have to send it back to my boss and say, 'Here's what I intend to do; what do you think?' He may have to run the idea up the chain of command even further! Then he'll come back and say, 'This is the one I choose for you.' Then I have to develop that option—and send it up to my boss for approval again! It comes back with his changes . . . and only then can you brief your people. All this time the platoon is milling around, trying to get organized for something—but they aren't at all sure just what it will be.

"This kind of micro-management is the sort of thing we were getting into down in Panama. We were getting into operations where we required outside people, who weren't on the ground with us, telling us how we were going to do things, based on our written plan—asking for permission, which is asking for trouble.

"We tend to do more of our planning now for somebody else, rather than for the teams, to demonstrate that we know how to do something when we're evaluated by our higher authority, or in an exercise where we're demonstrating to an umpire that we're doing things according to doctrine. If you were to take that

same platoon and turn them out into an op area for six months where they eat, breathe, and live in the area, like we did on the barges in the Persian Gulf during the Iran-Iraq War, pretty soon you fall into the old habits. You know your operations area, you know your platoon—you go back to basics. You plan your operation on the basis of the lowest common denominator and use the KISS principle [keep it simple, stupid!]. That way you have fewer things go wrong, you have a simpler operation to run, you rely on your knowledge of your platoon to deal with contingencies. That's called *flexibility*."

SEAL Virtues & Vices

"We're quite good at maritime direct action missions—where we ourselves are out there, in the water, delivering the munitions, collecting reconnaissance. Second, we are capable of doing long-range, long-duration missions—but we haven't typically been very good at it. The reason is that when you do these long missions, with all their logistics support requirements, you lose the ability to be fast, light, mobile. The minute you start putting on hundred-pound packs you lose that ability to do what we've traditionally done best."

The Training Environment Vs. the Real World

"I see a lot of guys who just don't get serious about our business. People have a tendency in training, in noncombat exercises, to take shortcuts. We can't afford to do that in this business. The way that you train is the way that you fight. If you get used to taking shortcuts because it's not dangerous, you'll get killed by that shortcut out in the real world. The business that we do is inherently dangerous anyway—parachuting, diving with closed-circuit rigs, locking out of submarines, working with explosives, shooting close to each other—those things are dangerous, but there is a difference even between doing them in training and in combat.

"I cannot explain to somebody until they see it for themselves what it is like to have somebody fall down beside them with a bullet in them, blood coming out of them—to lose a friend—to explain to them that they are vulnerable. You feel like you are almost invincible until you see something like that—and you never get that same feeling in any exercise, no matter how tough we make it. It takes something like that to make you really get serious about this business.

"Because there aren't real bullets going by overhead, people today don't realize you don't go very far very fast in combat. We have a tendency today to say we can travel twelve nautical miles an hour—a figure that is only realistic in a noncombat environment. It was not unusual in Vietnam to take an hour to go 100 meters back then; you had noise control, mud to contend with, water up to your chest. A hundred meters in an hour was rather fast. But we typically expect much faster movement from our SEALs today.

"Another thing we need to learn is to stop carrying all this extra gear; lighter, faster, smaller is better! I see guys going out with 200 rounds—you don't need all that. You need to stay mobile, you need to stay light, you don't want to sink too deep in the mud. You need to go back to basics again . . . when you get in the real world.

"But when I left SEAL Team Three we had only five guys out of 205 people who ever had any combat time—and I'll bet that, out of those five guys, not all of them had ever seen anybody get hurt! So you've got five guys who are serious and about 200 who say, 'I like this job, it's neat, it's fun . . .' Years ago, when we had teams come back with ten of the fourteen guys on a platoon having been wounded, we had a lot of guys who said ' . . . Uh, look, I don't want to do this anymore, I think I'll get out.' We don't have that now because we don't have all those casualties."

Technology—A Blessing and a Curse

"Our weapons system, operating gear, and radios are all better now than ever before. Technology has helped us in many ways—but now, we tend to load up on this stuff, because

we have it. I've actually stopped people getting ready for an operation and had them weigh their packs—which turned out to weigh 110 pounds—for a three-day operation, and I say, 'What's wrong with this picture?' You don't need to do that! You need a couple of LRRPs [similar to MREs], enough water to get you by for that period, your weapon and ammunition—and *that's it.* Let's go! Batteries, maybe an extra radio, no more than that.

"We have a tendency today to do more 'whizbang' stuff—night vision sight systems, laser aim-point systems—it's smaller/lighter/faster today. If I had to go back over there today, I think we'd operate pretty much the same kind of ops. The radios are better now, the waterproofing is better.

"We don't have a tendency to move into an area and get to know it before an operation now, although the Persian Gulf was something of an exception. I think that's very important—you have to move into your area and become familiar with your territory. And we have a tendency to really overdo the briefings—I see briefings lasting five and six hours! It's ludicrous! A human being can't remember all that. When we're going out for a two-day operation, why do you need to brief for five or six hours? If you're working well together on the team, patrolling and training together, you're familiar with your op area and you know your guys, and you don't need to brief that long. Instead of briefing for the benefit of the senior commander present, I think we need to remember that you're briefing your *platoon.*"

Joint Operations and the Multi-service Environment

"In Vietnam, our boat support units lived with us in the same hut. I could go over to the next bunk and say, 'We're going on an op tomorrow night—can you have this boat ready to go?' *Nowadays* assets like boats are coordinated by multi-services. If I need a boat now, even though it's internal, I have to make sure everybody knows about it because somebody else may be planning to use the same boat—so

I have to go to higher authority, tell them I need this boat, get my ticket punched, *then* I can go over to the guy on the next bunk and talk to him about it. If it's a helicopter that could belong to the Air Force or the Army, I might have to go all the way up the chain of command, find out if it's okay, involve them in my planning process, make them part of the mission planning. Since I'm not living in my op area, I have to rely on higher headquarters to 'de-conflict' my mission, to make sure that they aren't sending an Army Green Beret A team into the same area, where we might end up shooting at each other.

"We used to be well-segregated from other friendly units in Vietnam. We all had our assigned AO [Area of Operations], and you didn't cross over without checking with the other team. The same thing applied to the boat units—I could go to the riverine boat comman- der and say, 'You guys working in here? No? Well, we are, and I don't want you going in there with your boats now.' Nowadays you can't do it that simple."

Parachute Operations for Seals

"The rule for parachute operations is: If you *have* to jump, go find another way; if you still can't find another way, make sure you observe the restrictions on wind speed, weights, all that. We have a tendency to make things more complicated than they need to be—we should always go to the lowest common denominator. We have a tendency to send more people than we need when instead we ought to take the minimum. That makes for much better command and control. We get into trouble, as in Grenada and Panama, when we make things too complex."

One Foot in the Water

Special ops is a kind of military art form, a team sport that takes special talents and years to learn. Despite overlap of missions and training, each American special forces unit has a limited set of talents. For the SEALs, that means missions that are somehow linked to the sea. As one SEAL team commander explains, "The US military has Green Berets that dive, US Army Rangers that do across-the-beach operations with the same kind of Combat Rubber Raiding Craft that SEALs use—there are lots of similar examples in the Army and Marine Corps. We in the SEALs are the United States military's *small unit maritime special operations force*. We don't operate in larger than sixteen-man units. We don't belong in anything that involves multi-platoon operations—we've never been successful at it, we've never trained in it, and any time we've tried it we have failed. We keep our units small and separate from large force operations.

We have a niche there to be very good, in units most often less than eight men. That makes us harder to detect, easier to command and control, better at the small, unique operations that we train for. The Green Berets may conduct dive operations to get to their objective; we can conduct operations entirely underwater. US Army Rangers conduct large unit across-the-beach operations, and it isn't unusual to see them use twelve or more CRRCs. You probably will never see more than two in our business.

"We keep one foot in the water. That means that *if* we must do inland operations it is because they are attached to some maritime reason—that was the only available insertion technique, or it happens to be a coastal target. *Keeping one foot in the water* means that we don't get into areas that properly belong to other operators."

Index